Mastering PHP 7: A Comprehensive Guide to Modern Web Development

Kameron Hussain and Frahaan Hussain

Published by Sonar Publishing, 2024.

MASTERING PHP 7: A COMPREHENSIVE GUIDE TO MODERN WEB DEVELOPMENT

First edition. January 25, 2024.

ISBN: 979-8224125586

Written by Kameron Hussain and Frahaan Hussain.

Table of Contents

Conclusion

Section 11.4: Cross-Platform Development with PHP

Using PHP for Backend Services

Cross-Platform Development Frameworks

Example of Cross-Platform App Development

Section 11.5: Performance Optimization for Mobile Apps

1. Caching: Implement caching mechanisms to reduce server load and minimize data transfer between the mobile app and the PHP backend. Use technologies like Memcached or Redis to store frequently accessed data, such as API responses, database query results, and images.

2. Optimized API Endpoints: Design your API endpoints to return only the necessary data and avoid over-fetching. Use pagination and filtering to limit the amount of data transmitted. Minimize the use of large payloads in API responses, especially for mobile networks.

3. Code Profiling: Profile your PHP code to identify performance bottlenecks. Tools like Xdebug and Blackfire Profiler can help pinpoint areas that require optimization. Optimize database queries, reduce unnecessary function calls, and optimize loops.

4. Image Compression: Compress images to reduce their file sizes before serving them to mobile devices. Use image

optimization libraries or services to ensure that images are appropriately sized and formatted for mobile screens.

5. Minification and Bundling: Minify JavaScript and CSS files to reduce their size. Bundle multiple files into one to minimize the number of HTTP requests made by the mobile app. Tools like UglifyJS and CSS minifiers can help with this.

6. Lazy Loading: Implement lazy loading for resources such as images and videos. Load content only when it's visible to the user, reducing the initial load time of your mobile app.

7. Background Processing: Offload resource-intensive tasks, such as image processing or data synchronization, to background processes. Use tools like Gearman or RabbitMQ to queue and process tasks asynchronously.

8. Network Optimization: Minimize the number of network requests made by your mobile app. Combine API requests, use HTTP/2 for faster loading, and enable GZIP compression on the server to reduce data transfer.

9. Resource Management: Manage memory and resources efficiently in your PHP code. Release unused resources, close database connections after use, and avoid memory leaks.

10. Testing and Profiling: Continuously test your mobile app's performance on real devices and use profiling tools to identify and address performance issues as they arise. Monitor server resource usage to ensure optimal performance.

5. Two-Factor Authentication (2FA)

6. Regular Security Audits

7. Secure Coding Practices

8. Data Encryption

9. User Data Protection

10. Regular Updates

11. Incident Response Plan

12. Security Training

Section 14.5: Analyzing and Optimizing E-commerce Performance

1. Performance Metrics

2. Caching

3. Content Delivery Network (CDN)

4. Lazy Loading

5. Database Optimization

6. Minification and Compression

7. Mobile Optimization

8. Load Testing

9. Code Profiling

10. Content Optimization

11. Content Preloading

Chapter 1: Introduction to PHP 7

1.1 Evolution of PHP: From Early Days to PHP 7

PHP (Hypertext Preprocessor) has come a long way since its inception. It began as a simple scripting language for web development and has evolved into a powerful server-side scripting language widely used for building dynamic web applications. In this section, we'll delve into the fascinating journey of PHP, from its early days to the robust PHP 7.

Early Days of PHP

PHP was created in 1994 by Rasmus Lerdorf as a set of Common Gateway Interface (CGI) binaries written in C. Its primary purpose was to track visits to his online resume. Initially, PHP stood for "Personal Home Page," but it later became known as "PHP: Hypertext Preprocessor," reflecting its expanded capabilities.

PHP 3: The First Milestone

PHP 3, released in 1998, marked a significant turning point. It introduced support for web forms, which allowed developers to create interactive web applications. The addition of support for databases, including MySQL, further enhanced PHP's capabilities, making it a popular choice for web development.

PHP 4: Gaining Popularity

PHP 4, released in 2000, brought substantial improvements. It featured an integrated scripting engine and introduced support for object-oriented programming (OOP) with the introduction of classes and objects. PHP 4 quickly gained popularity and became the foundation for many web applications.

PHP 5: The Birth of Modern PHP

PHP 5, released in 2004, was a game-changer. It introduced the Zend Engine 2.0, offering significant performance enhancements. This version embraced OOP principles more fully, making PHP a more robust and maintainable language. The introduction of features like exceptions and improved support for XML further solidified PHP's position in web development.

The PHP 6 Saga

PHP 6 was initially in development to bring native support for Unicode. However, due to various technical challenges and delays, PHP 6 was never officially released. The community moved on to PHP 5.3 and later versions.

PHP 7: A Leap Forward

PHP 7, released in December 2015, is a significant milestone in PHP's history. It brought substantial performance improvements, making PHP applications run significantly faster. The introduction of the PHPNG (PHP Next-Gen) engine played a pivotal role in this performance boost.

PHP 7 also introduced new language features and improvements, including the spaceship operator (<=>) for easy value comparisons, scalar type declarations, return type declarations, and more. These enhancements made PHP more modern and developer-friendly.

In conclusion, PHP has evolved from a simple web scripting language into a powerful, feature-rich platform for web development. PHP 7, with its performance enhancements and new features, has solidified its position as a leading choice for building dynamic web applications.

Remember, this is just the beginning of our exploration into PHP 7, and there's much more to discover in the subsequent chapters of this book. Let's dive deeper into the key features and improvements PHP 7 brings to the table in the following sections.

1.2 Key Features and Improvements in PHP 7

PHP 7 introduced several key features and improvements over its predecessors, making it a more robust and efficient programming language for web development. In this section, we'll explore some of the most significant enhancements that PHP 7 brings to the table.

1. Significant Performance Boost

One of the most remarkable improvements in PHP 7 is its significant performance boost. The introduction of the PHPNG (PHP Next-Gen) engine resulted in a considerable reduction in memory consumption and a substantial increase in execution speed. PHP 7 can execute your code up to twice as fast as PHP 5.6, making it a compelling choice for high-performance web applications.

```
// PHP 5.6

$start = microtime(true);

for ($i = 0; $i < 1000000; $i++) {

// Your code here

}

$end = microtime(true);
```

```
echo "Execution time: " . ($end - $start) . " seconds";

// PHP 7

$start = microtime(true);

for ($i = 0; $i < 1000000; $i++) {

// Your code here

}

$end = microtime(true);

echo "Execution time: " . ($end - $start) . " seconds";
```

2. Scalar Type Declarations

PHP 7 introduced scalar type declarations, allowing you to specify the expected data type of function parameters and return values. This helps improve code reliability and makes it easier to catch type-related errors during development.

```
// PHP 7

function add(int $a, int $b): int {

return $a + $b;

}

$result = add(5, 10); // Result is guaranteed to be an integer
```

3. Return Type Declarations

In addition to parameter type declarations, PHP 7 also introduced return type declarations, allowing you to specify the expected return type of functions. This enhances code readability and helps prevent unexpected return values.

```
// PHP 7

function divide(float $a, float $b): float {

return $a / $b;

}

$result = divide(10.0, 2.0); // Result is guaranteed to be a float
```

4. Null Coalescing Operator

The null coalescing operator (??) is a convenient addition to PHP 7. It allows you to provide a default value if a variable is null, reducing the need for verbose conditional statements.

```
// PHP 7

$username = $_GET['username'] ?? 'Guest';
```

5. Spaceship Operator

The spaceship operator (<=>) introduced in PHP 7 simplifies value comparisons by returning -1, 0, or 1 based on the comparison result. This operator is particularly useful for sorting and custom comparison functions.

```
// PHP 7

$result = $value1 <=> $value2;
```

6. Anonymous Classes

PHP 7 introduced support for anonymous classes, allowing you to create simple, one-off classes without specifying a name. This can be handy for quick object instantiation.

```
// PHP 7

$object = new class {

public function sayHello() {

echo "Hello, anonymous class!";

}

};

$object->sayHello();
```

7. Error Handling Improvements

PHP 7 improved error handling with the introduction of the Throwable interface. This interface serves as the base for both exceptions and errors, providing a unified way to handle both in your code.

```
// PHP 7

try {

// Code that may throw an exception or error

} catch (Throwable $e) {

// Handle the exception or error

}
```

These are just a few of the key features and improvements introduced in PHP 7. As we proceed through this book, you'll have the opportunity to explore these and many more features in greater depth, helping you become a proficient PHP developer.

1.3 Setting Up the Development Environment

Setting up a proper development environment is a crucial step when working with PHP 7. A well-configured environment ensures that you can efficiently develop, test, and debug your PHP applications. In this section, we'll guide you through the process of setting up your PHP 7 development environment.

1. Installing PHP 7

Before you can start developing with PHP 7, you need to install it on your system. PHP 7 can be easily installed on various operating systems. Below are some common installation methods:

- **Linux:** You can use your package manager to install PHP 7. For example, on Ubuntu, you can run sudo apt-get install php7.4 to install PHP 7.4.

- **Windows:** You can download the official PHP distribution for Windows from the PHP website and follow the installation instructions.

- **macOS:** macOS comes with PHP pre-installed, but you can use package managers like Homebrew to install a specific PHP version.

2. Choosing a Text Editor or IDE

Selecting the right text editor or integrated development environment (IDE) is essential for efficient PHP development. Some popular choices for PHP development include:

- **Visual Studio Code (VS Code):** A lightweight and highly extensible code editor with excellent PHP support through extensions like PHP Intelephense.

- **PHPStorm:** A robust PHP-specific IDE with features like code completion, debugging, and integrated support for PHP tools and frameworks.

- **NetBeans:** An open-source IDE with strong PHP support, providing features like code templates, code navigation, and debugging.

Choose an editor or IDE that suits your preferences and workflow. Make sure to configure it to work seamlessly with PHP by installing relevant extensions or plugins.

3. Setting Up a Local Development Server

To test your PHP applications locally, you'll need a web server and a database server. One of the most common setups for local development is using:

- **Apache or Nginx:** These web servers can serve PHP files locally. You can install them separately or use pre-configured packages like XAMPP or WAMP for Windows or MAMP for macOS.

- **MySQL or MariaDB:** These relational database management systems are widely used with PHP applications. Install and configure one of them to store and retrieve data.

4. Version Control System (VCS)

Using a version control system like Git is essential for tracking changes in your code and collaborating with other developers. Create a Git repository for your PHP project and regularly commit your code to keep a history of changes.

5. Dependency Management

Dependency management tools like Composer are crucial for managing external libraries and packages in your PHP project. Composer simplifies the process of including third-party libraries and frameworks into your application.

```
# Install Composer globally (Linux/macOS)

curl -sS https://getcomposer.org/installer | php

sudo mv composer.phar /usr/local/bin/composer
```

6. Testing Tools

Consider using testing tools like PHPUnit to write and run tests for your PHP code. Testing helps ensure the reliability and stability of your applications.

```
// Example PHPUnit test

public function testAddition() {

$result = add(5, 10);

$this->assertEquals(15, $result);
```

```
}
```

7. Debugging Tools

Debugging is a crucial part of development. PHP offers built-in debugging features, and you can also use third-party tools like Xdebug to enhance your debugging capabilities.

8. Documentation

Keep your code well-documented using comments and follow PHPDoc standards. Tools like phpDocumentor can generate documentation from your codebase, making it easier for you and others to understand and use your code.

Setting up a development environment is an essential foundation for PHP development. A well-configured environment ensures that you can work efficiently, collaborate effectively, and produce high-quality PHP applications. Take the time to set up your environment correctly, and you'll be on your way to becoming a proficient PHP developer.

1.4 Basic Syntax and Structure of PHP 7

Understanding the basic syntax and structure of PHP 7 is fundamental to becoming proficient in PHP development. In this section, we'll explore the core elements of PHP code, including variables, data types, operators, and control structures.

1. PHP Tags

In PHP, you enclose your code within PHP tags. The standard PHP opening tag is <?php, and the closing tag is ?>. For example:

```
<?php
```

```
// Your PHP code goes here

?>
```

2. Outputting Text

To display text or content to the browser, you can use the echo or print statements. These statements are often used to output HTML content along with PHP variables.

```
<?php

$message = "Hello, PHP!";

echo $message;

// Output: Hello, PHP!

?>
```

3. Variables and Data Types

In PHP, you can create variables to store data. Variables are preceded by a $ symbol, followed by the variable name. PHP supports various data types, including integers, floats, strings, booleans, arrays, and objects.

```
<?php

$integerVar = 42;

$floatVar = 3.14;

$stringVar = "Hello, World!";

$booleanVar = true;

$arrayVar = [1, 2, 3];
```

```
$objectVar = new MyClass();

?>
```

4. Comments

You can add comments to your PHP code to provide explanations or notes. PHP supports both single-line and multi-line comments.

```
<?php

// This is a single-line comment

/*

This is a

multi-line comment

*/

?>
```

5. Operators

PHP offers various operators for performing operations on data. Some common operators include arithmetic operators (+, -, *, /), assignment operators (=, +=, -=), comparison operators (==, !=, <, >), and logical operators (&&, ||, !).

```
<?php

$a = 10;

$b = 5;

$sum = $a + $b; // Addition
```

```
$difference = $a - $b; // Subtraction

$product = $a * $b; // Multiplication

$quotient = $a / $b; // Division

$isEqual = ($a == $b); // Comparison

$logicalResult = ($a > 5) && ($b < 7); // Logical operation

?>
```

6. Strings

PHP provides robust support for working with strings. You can concatenate strings using the . operator, and you can use double-quoted or single-quoted strings.

```
<?php

$name = "John";

$greeting = "Hello, " . $name . "!";

echo $greeting;

// Output: Hello, John!

?>
```

7. Control Structures

PHP offers various control structures for making decisions and repeating actions. Common control structures include:

- **Conditional Statements:** if, else if, else, and the switch statement.

```
<?php
$num = 10;
if ($num > 0) {
echo "Positive";
} else if ($num < 0) {
echo "Negative";
} else {
echo "Zero";
}
?>
```

- **Loops:** for, while, do-while, and foreach loops.

```
<?php
// For loop
for ($i = 0; $i < 5; $i++) {
echo $i;
}
// While loop
$counter = 0;
while ($counter < 3) {
echo $counter;
```

```
$counter++;
}
?>
```

Understanding these basic elements of PHP syntax and structure is crucial as they form the building blocks for creating more complex PHP applications. As you progress in your PHP journey, you'll combine these elements to create dynamic and interactive web applications.

1.5 Transitioning from Older Versions to PHP 7

If you have experience with older versions of PHP, transitioning to PHP 7 may require some adjustments due to the language's evolution. In this section, we'll explore the key considerations and steps for transitioning from older PHP versions to PHP 7.

1. Compatibility Checking

Before migrating to PHP 7, it's essential to assess the compatibility of your existing codebase. Start by identifying any deprecated functions or features that may not work in PHP 7. PHP provides documentation that lists deprecated features for each version, making it easier to identify potential issues.

2. Updating Deprecated Code

Once you've identified deprecated code in your application, update it to use modern alternatives. For example, PHP 7 introduced the null coalescing operator (??) as a replacement for some uses of the ternary operator (? :) with isset(). Updating your codebase to use the new operator improves readability and maintainability.

3. Checking for Error Handling

PHP 7 introduced changes in error handling. The error_reporting() function and error levels have been updated. Review your error handling mechanisms and adjust them to align with PHP 7's error reporting standards.

4. Type Declarations

PHP 7 introduced scalar type declarations (int, float, string, and bool) and return type declarations. While these are optional, consider adding them to your functions and methods for improved code clarity and type safety.

5. Namespaces and Autoloading

Ensure that your code uses namespaces and follows modern autoloading practices. Namespaces help prevent naming conflicts, and autoloading simplifies the inclusion of class files. Both are essential for organizing and maintaining large codebases.

6. Updating MySQL Extensions

If your application uses the older MySQL extension (mysql_* functions), consider migrating to either the MySQLi or PDO extension. PHP 7 deprecated the MySQL extension, and it's no longer available in PHP 7.0 and later versions.

7. Updating PHP Extensions

Check the compatibility of third-party PHP extensions or libraries you use in your application. Some extensions may need updates to work correctly with PHP 7. Ensure you have the latest versions installed.

8. Testing and Quality Assurance

Thoroughly test your application after making code changes to ensure it functions correctly in a PHP 7 environment. Automated testing tools like PHPUnit can help identify and fix issues efficiently.

9. Performance Optimization

Take advantage of PHP 7's improved performance by optimizing your code where necessary. Review database queries, improve algorithm efficiency, and consider using opcode caching solutions like OPCache.

10. Upgrading PHP Version

Finally, update your server or hosting environment to PHP 7 or a later version. Consult your hosting provider or system administrator for guidance on upgrading PHP. Keep in mind that PHP 5.6 reached its end of life, so transitioning to PHP 7 or later is essential for security and performance reasons.

By following these steps and ensuring your codebase is compatible with PHP 7, you can take full advantage of the language's improvements and keep your PHP applications up to date and secure.

Chapter 2: PHP 7 Fundamentals

2.1 Variables and Data Types

In PHP 7, understanding variables and data types is foundational for writing effective code. Variables allow you to store and manipulate data, while data types define the kind of data that can be stored in a variable. Let's dive into the fundamentals of variables and data types in PHP 7.

Variables in PHP

In PHP, you declare variables using the $ symbol followed by a variable name. Variable names are case-sensitive and can consist of letters, numbers, and underscores. Here's how you declare and assign values to variables:

$age = 30; *// Assigning an integer value*

$name = "John"; *// Assigning a string value*

$isStudent = **true**; *// Assigning a boolean value*

Data Types in PHP

PHP supports several data types, including:

1. **Integers:** Represent whole numbers, positive or negative, without a decimal point. Example: $count = 42;
2. **Floats (Doubles):** Represent numbers with a decimal point or in exponential form. Example: $price = 5.99;
3. **Strings:** Represent sequences of characters enclosed in single or double quotes. Example: $name = "Alice";
4. **Booleans:** Represent true or false values. Example:

$isApproved = true;

5. **Arrays:** Collections of values, including indexed arrays and associative arrays. Example:

```
$fruits = array("apple", "banana", "cherry");

$person = array("name" => "John", "age" => 30);
```

1. **Objects:** Instances of user-defined classes or built-in classes in PHP. Example:

```
class Car {

public $brand;

public $model;

}

$myCar = new Car();

$myCar->brand = "Toyota";
```

1. **NULL:** Represents the absence of a value. Example: $noValue = null;

Variable Naming Conventions

When naming variables in PHP, it's essential to follow some conventions:

- Variable names should start with a letter or an underscore.
- Variable names cannot start with a number.

- Variable names are case-sensitive, so $count and $Count are considered different variables.
- Use meaningful and descriptive names to make your code more readable and maintainable.

Variable Scope

Variables in PHP have different scopes, which determine where they can be accessed:

- **Local Scope:** Variables declared inside a function have local scope and are only accessible within that function.
- **Global Scope:** Variables declared outside of any function have global scope and can be accessed throughout the entire script.

```
$globalVar = 10; // Global variable

function myFunction() {

$localVar = 5; // Local variable

echo $globalVar; // Accessing a global variable within a function

}

myFunction();

echo $localVar; // This will result in an error, as $localVar is not accessible here.
```

Understanding variables and data types is the foundation for working with PHP. As you continue your journey in PHP development, you'll use variables to store and manipulate data, and you'll leverage different data types to handle various kinds of information in your applications.

2.2 Control Structures: Loops and Conditional Statements

Control structures, including loops and conditional statements, are essential tools in PHP for controlling the flow of your code and making decisions. In this section, we'll explore the use of loops and conditional statements in PHP 7.

Conditional Statements

Conditional statements allow you to execute specific blocks of code based on whether a given condition is true or false. PHP provides several conditional statements, including:

if Statement

The if statement is used to execute a block of code if a specified condition is true.

```
$age = 25;

if ($age >= 18) {

echo "You are an adult.";

} else {

echo "You are a minor.";

}
```

else if Statement

You can use the else if statement to test multiple conditions sequentially.

```
$grade = 75;

if ($grade >= 90) {

echo "Excellent!";

} elseif ($grade >= 70) {

echo "Good!";

} else {

echo "Needs improvement.";

}
```

switch Statement

The switch statement is used to select one of many code blocks to be executed.

```
$day = "Wednesday";

switch ($day) {

case "Monday":

echo "It's the start of the week.";

break;

case "Wednesday":
```

```
echo "It's midweek!";

break;

default:

echo "It's some other day.";

}
```

Loops

Loops allow you to execute a block of code repeatedly until a specified condition is met. PHP provides several types of loops, including:

for Loop

The for loop is commonly used when you know how many times you want to repeat a block of code.

```
for ($i = 1; $i <= 5; $i++) {

echo "Iteration $i <br>";

}
```

while Loop

The while loop continues executing a block of code as long as a specified condition is true.

```
$counter = 1;

while ($counter <= 3) {

echo "Iteration $counter <br>";
```

```
$counter++;
}
```

do-while Loop

The do-while loop is similar to the while loop but guarantees that the code block is executed at least once before checking the condition.

```
$counter = 1;
do {
echo "Iteration $counter <br>";
$counter++;
} while ($counter <= 3);
```

foreach Loop

The foreach loop is specifically designed for iterating over arrays.

```
$fruits = ["apple", "banana", "cherry"];
foreach ($fruits as $fruit) {
echo "I like $fruit <br>";
}
```

Control structures are powerful tools for making your PHP code dynamic and responsive to different conditions and data. By mastering these concepts, you can create more sophisticated and interactive PHP applications.

2.3 Functions and Scope

Functions are a fundamental concept in PHP that allow you to encapsulate a block of code and reuse it throughout your application. In this section, we'll explore functions and their scope in PHP 7.

Creating Functions

To create a function in PHP, you use the function keyword, followed by the function name and a pair of parentheses. The function name must follow the same naming conventions as variables.

```
function sayHello() {

echo "Hello, World!";

}
```

You can call this function by using its name followed by parentheses:

```
sayHello(); // Output: Hello, World!
```

Function Parameters

Functions can accept parameters, which allow you to pass values into the function. Parameters are defined within the parentheses after the function name.

```
function greet($name) {

echo "Hello, $name!";

}

greet("Alice"); // Output: Hello, Alice!
```

You can define multiple parameters by separating them with commas:

```
function add($a, $b) {

return $a + $b;

}

$result = add(5, 3); // $result will be 8
```

Return Values

Functions can return values using the return statement. This allows you to compute a value within the function and then use that result elsewhere in your code.

```
function multiply($x, $y) {

return $x * $y;

}

$product = multiply(4, 6); // $product will be 24
```

Function Scope

PHP has both global scope and local scope for variables. Variables declared within a function have local scope and are only accessible within that function. Variables declared outside of any function have global scope and can be accessed throughout the entire script.

```
$globalVar = 10; // Global variable

function myFunction() {

$localVar = 5; // Local variable
```

```
echo $localVar;

echo $globalVar; // Accessing a global variable within a function

}

myFunction();

echo $globalVar; // Accessing a global variable outside of the function
```

The global Keyword

To access global variables within a function, you can use the global keyword followed by the variable name.

```
$globalVar = 10; // Global variable

function myFunction() {

global $globalVar;

echo $globalVar; // Accessing a global variable using the global keyword

}

myFunction();
```

Static Variables

Static variables retain their value between function calls. You can declare a static variable using the static keyword.

```
function increment() {

static $counter = 0; // Static variable

$counter++;
```

```
echo $counter;
}
increment(); // Output: 1
increment(); // Output: 2
increment(); // Output: 3
```

Understanding functions and scope is crucial for organizing and modularizing your PHP code. Functions allow you to break your code into manageable pieces and promote code reuse, making your applications more maintainable and efficient.

2.4 Error Handling in PHP 7

Error handling is a critical aspect of PHP development, ensuring that your code can gracefully handle unexpected situations and failures. In PHP 7, there are various techniques and functions available for error handling. In this section, we'll explore these methods to help you write robust and reliable PHP applications.

Error Reporting

PHP provides the error_reporting() function to control which types of errors are reported and displayed. You can use this function to set the error reporting level, allowing you to customize how PHP handles errors.

```
error_reporting(E_ERROR | E_WARNING); // Report only errors and warnings
```

The above code sets the error reporting level to display only errors and warnings. This is useful for development environments where you want to catch and fix issues early.

Error Types

PHP categorizes errors into different types, including:

- **E_ERROR:** Fatal runtime errors that terminate script execution.
- **E_WARNING:** Non-fatal runtime errors that don't terminate script execution but should be addressed.
- **E_NOTICE:** Non-critical runtime notices.
- **E_PARSE:** Compile-time parse errors.
- **E_DEPRECATED:** Notices for deprecated features.
- **E_STRICT:** Suggests changes to code that might ensure forward compatibility.

Handling Errors

try...catch Blocks

PHP supports exception handling using try...catch blocks. You can use these blocks to catch and handle exceptions gracefully, preventing script termination.

```
try {
// Code that may throw an exception
$result = 10 / 0; // This will throw a DivisionByZeroError
} catch (DivisionByZeroError $e) {
echo "Error: Division by zero";
```

}

Custom Error Handlers

PHP allows you to define custom error handlers using the set_error_handler() function. This enables you to handle errors in a way that suits your application.

```
function customErrorHandler($errno, $errstr, $errfile, $errline) {
echo "Custom Error: [$errno] $errstr in $errfile on line $errline<br>";
}
// Set the custom error handler
set_error_handler("customErrorHandler");
// Trigger a custom error
echo $undefinedVariable; // This will trigger the customErrorHandler
```

Logging Errors

In production environments, it's common to log errors to a file instead of displaying them on the screen. You can configure PHP to log errors by setting the error_log directive in the php.ini file.

```
error_log("This error is logged to a file.");
```

Exception Handling

In PHP, you can throw exceptions using the throw statement and catch them using try...catch blocks. This is particularly useful when you encounter exceptional situations in your code.

```
function divide($a, $b) {

if ($b == 0) {

throw new Exception("Division by zero is not allowed.");

}

return $a / $b;

}

try {

$result = divide(10, 0);

echo "Result: $result";

} catch (Exception $e) {

echo "Error: " . $e->getMessage();

}
```

By implementing proper error and exception handling, you can make your PHP applications more robust and user-friendly. Effective error handling ensures that issues are identified and addressed promptly, improving the overall reliability of your code.

2.5 Best Practices in Coding Standards

Maintaining a consistent and clean coding style is essential for writing readable, maintainable, and collaborative PHP code. In this section, we'll explore some best practices and coding standards commonly followed by PHP developers.

1. PSR Standards

The PHP-FIG (PHP Framework Interop Group) has established a set of coding standards known as PSR (PHP Standard Recommendation) standards. These standards define conventions for file and class naming, coding style, and autoloading. Following these standards ensures consistency across PHP projects and facilitates code sharing between developers.

- **PSR-1:** Basic coding standard with guidelines for class and file names, namespaces, and code structure.

- **PSR-2:** Coding style guide with rules for indentation, brace placement, whitespace, and more.

- **PSR-4:** Autoloading standard for namespaces, specifying how classes should be autoloaded.

2. Naming Conventions

- Use meaningful and descriptive names for variables, functions, classes, and methods.

- Follow camelCase naming for variables and functions (e.g., $userName, calculateTotal()).

- Use PascalCase naming for class names (e.g., MyClass, DatabaseConnection).

• Prefix abstract classes with "Abstract" (e.g., AbstractController).

3. Indentation and Whitespace

• Use consistent indentation (typically four spaces) to enhance code readability.

• Avoid trailing whitespace at the end of lines.

• Use one blank line to separate logical sections of code for clarity.

4. Comments and Documentation

• Add meaningful comments to explain complex code, algorithms, or any non-obvious logic.

• Use PHPDoc comments to document classes, methods, and function signatures.

• Describe parameters, return values, and exceptions in PHPDoc comments for clarity.

```
/**
* Calculate the total price.
*
* @param float $price The base price.
* @param int $quantity The quantity of items.
* @return float The total price.
```

```
*/
function calculateTotal($price, $quantity) {
// Calculate the total price
return $price * $quantity;
}
```

5. Error Handling

- Implement proper error and exception handling to gracefully handle errors and exceptions.
- Avoid using die(), exit(), or similar functions for error handling in production code.
- Log errors and exceptions for debugging purposes and monitor logs in production.

6. Code Reusability

- Promote code reusability by breaking code into functions and classes.
- Use inheritance and composition to structure code and promote modularity.
- Avoid duplicating code; instead, create reusable functions or methods.

7. Security Practices

- Sanitize user input to prevent SQL injection, cross-site scripting (XSS), and other security vulnerabilities.

- Use prepared statements when interacting with databases to prevent SQL injection.

- Keep sensitive information (e.g., database credentials) in configuration files outside of the web root.

8. Version Control

- Utilize version control systems like Git to track changes, collaborate with others, and maintain a history of your code.

- Follow branching and merging best practices when working on collaborative projects.

9. Testing

- Implement unit testing using frameworks like PHPUnit to ensure the correctness of your code.

- Write test cases to cover various code paths and edge cases.

Adhering to these coding standards and best practices not only improves the quality of your PHP code but also makes it easier for you and your team to work on projects efficiently. Consistency in coding style and practices simplifies code maintenance and enhances the overall quality of your PHP applications.

Chapter 3: Advanced PHP 7 Concepts

3.1 Object-Oriented Programming in PHP 7

Object-Oriented Programming (OOP) is a powerful paradigm in PHP 7 that allows you to model real-world entities and their interactions in your applications. OOP promotes code reusability, modularity, and maintainability. In this section, we'll delve into the principles of OOP in PHP 7.

Classes and Objects

In PHP, classes are blueprints for creating objects. A class defines the properties (attributes) and methods (functions) that objects of that class will have. Here's an example of defining a simple class:

```
class Car {

// Properties (attributes)

public $brand;

public $model;

// Methods (functions)

public function startEngine() {

echo "Engine started!";

}

}
```

You can create objects (instances) of the Car class as follows:

```
$myCar = new Car();

$myCar->brand = "Toyota";

$myCar->model = "Camry";
```

Encapsulation

Encapsulation is one of the core principles of OOP. It involves bundling data (properties) and the methods (functions) that operate on that data within a single unit called a class. Encapsulation helps in controlling access to an object's data, allowing you to define public, protected, and private properties and methods.

- **Public:** Public properties and methods can be accessed from anywhere, both within and outside the class.
- **Protected:** Protected properties and methods can only be accessed within the class and its subclasses (inheritance).
- **Private:** Private properties and methods are restricted to the class they are defined in.

```
class Student {

public $name; // Public property

protected $age; // Protected property

private $grade; // Private property

public function __construct($name, $age, $grade) {

$this->name = $name;

$this->age = $age;
```

```
$this->grade = $grade;
}
}
```

Inheritance

Inheritance allows you to create a new class (subclass or derived class) based on an existing class (base class or parent class). The subclass inherits the properties and methods of the parent class and can also have its own additional properties and methods.

```
class Animal {
public $species;
public function __construct($species) {
$this->species = $species;
}
public function speak() {
echo "Animal speaks!";
}
}
class Dog extends Animal {
public function speak() {
echo "Woof!";
}
```

```
}
```

Polymorphism

Polymorphism allows objects of different classes to be treated as objects of a common superclass. This allows for flexibility in code design and can simplify complex systems.

```
class Shape {
public function calculateArea() {
// Default implementation
}
}
class Circle extends Shape {
public $radius;
public function calculateArea() {
return 3.14 * $this->radius * $this->radius;
}
}
class Square extends Shape {
public $side;
public function calculateArea() {
return $this->side * $this->side;
}
```

```
}
```

Abstraction

Abstraction involves defining the essential characteristics of an object while hiding the unnecessary details. Abstract classes and methods are used to create a blueprint for other classes and ensure that specific methods are implemented in the subclasses.

```
abstract class Shape {

abstract public function calculateArea();

}

class Circle extends Shape {

public $radius;

public function calculateArea() {

return 3.14 * $this->radius * $this->radius;

}

}

class Square extends Shape {

public $side;

public function calculateArea() {

return $this->side * $this->side;

}

}
```

Object-Oriented Programming in PHP 7 enables you to design more structured and organized applications. By leveraging classes, inheritance, encapsulation, polymorphism, and abstraction, you can create efficient and maintainable code that is easier to extend and scale as your project evolves.

3.2 Namespaces and Autoloading

Namespaces and autoloading are essential concepts in PHP 7 that help organize and manage code in larger projects, prevent naming conflicts, and simplify class loading. In this section, we'll explore how namespaces and autoloading work in PHP.

Namespaces

Namespaces provide a way to organize and group related classes, functions, and constants into separate logical containers. This prevents naming conflicts when different libraries or packages use similar class names. A namespace is declared using the namespace keyword.

```
namespace MyApp;

class MyClass {

// Class definition

}
```

In the above example, the MyClass class belongs to the MyApp namespace.

Using Namespaces

You can use the use statement to import classes from a specific namespace, making it easier to access them in your code. This is especially useful when working with classes from different namespaces.

```
use MyApp\MyClass;
$obj = new MyClass();
```

Alias in Namespaces

You can also alias namespaces or classes with a different name to avoid conflicts or for brevity.

```
use MyApp\MyClass as CustomClass;
$obj = new CustomClass();
```

Global Namespace

Classes without a namespace declaration belong to the global namespace. You can access them directly or use a backslash (\) to denote the global namespace.

```
$object1 = new \MyClass(); // Accessing a class from the global namespace
$object2 = new MyClass(); // Assuming MyClass is in the global namespace
```

Autoloading

Autoloading is the process of automatically loading classes when they are used, eliminating the need to include or require class files manually. In PHP 7, the recommended way to implement autoloading is by using the spl_autoload_register() function.

```
spl_autoload_register(function ($className) {
// Convert class name to a file path and include it
include 'path/to/classes/' . $className . '.php';
});
```

The above code registers an autoloader that includes class files based on the class name and a predefined file structure.

Composer Autoloading

Composer, a popular PHP dependency manager, provides a powerful autoloading mechanism. When you include Composer in your project and define the autoloading rules in the composer.json file, it generates an autoloader for your classes.

```
{
"autoload": {
"psr-4": {
"MyApp\\": "src/"
}
}
}
```

In this example, the psr-4 autoloading standard is used to map the MyApp namespace to the src/ directory. Composer automatically generates an efficient autoloader based on these rules.

PSR-4 Autoloading

PSR-4 is a widely adopted autoloading standard that specifies a simple and efficient way to autoload classes based on namespaces. By following PSR-4 conventions, you can organize your class files in a directory structure that directly reflects the namespace hierarchy.

```
namespace MyApp;

class MyClass {

// Class definition

}
```

With PSR-4 autoloading, the class file for MyClass should be located at src/MyApp/MyClass.php, and Composer will automatically load it when needed.

Namespaces and autoloading are crucial tools for managing code organization and class loading in modern PHP development. They promote code reusability, prevent naming conflicts, and simplify the process of including classes in your projects.

3.3 Advanced Error Handling Techniques

In addition to basic error handling techniques discussed earlier, PHP 7 provides more advanced error handling mechanisms that can enhance the debugging and stability of your applications. In this section, we'll explore some of these advanced error handling techniques.

Custom Error Handlers

Custom error handlers offer greater control over how errors are handled in your PHP applications. You can define your own error handler functions using the set_error_handler() function. This allows you to log errors, send notifications, or take specific actions when errors occur.

```
function customErrorHandler($errno, $errstr, $errfile, $errline) {

// Custom error handling logic

echo "Error: [$errno] $errstr in $errfile on line $errline<br>";

}

// Set the custom error handler

set_error_handler("customErrorHandler");
```

With a custom error handler in place, you can customize error messages and responses to better suit your application's needs.

Exception Handling Strategies

Exception handling in PHP goes beyond basic try...catch blocks. Here are some advanced exception handling techniques:

Multiple Catch Blocks

You can use multiple catch blocks to handle different types of exceptions separately. This allows you to provide more specific error handling for various exceptional situations.

```
try {

// Code that may throw different exceptions

} catch (ExceptionType1 $e) {

// Handle ExceptionType1
```

```
} catch (ExceptionType2 $e) {
// Handle ExceptionType2
}
```

Rethrowing Exceptions

Sometimes, you may want to catch an exception, perform some operations, and then rethrow the same exception. This can be useful for logging, debugging, or adding additional context to the exception.

```
try {
// Code that may throw an exception
} catch (Exception $e) {
// Log the exception
error_log($e->getMessage());
// Re-throw the exception for further handling
throw $e;
}
```

Exception Chaining

You can chain exceptions by passing the previous exception as the third argument to a new exception's constructor. This preserves the original exception's stack trace and context.

```
try {
```

```
// Code that may throw an exception
} catch (Exception $e) {
// Create a new exception with the original exception as the previous exception
throw new CustomException("Custom error message", 0, $e);
}
```

Custom Exception Classes

Creating custom exception classes allows you to define specific exception types for your application. This makes error handling and debugging more straightforward, as you can catch and handle specific exceptions based on their types.

```
class MyCustomException extends Exception {
// Custom exception logic
}
try {
// Code that may throw MyCustomException
} catch (MyCustomException $e) {
// Handle MyCustomException
}
```

Error Suppression

The @ operator can be used to suppress errors or warnings generated by specific expressions or function calls. While it can be useful in certain cases, it's generally recommended to avoid using this operator, as it can make debugging and error resolution more challenging.

```
$result = @someFunction(); // Suppress errors, not recommended
```

Advanced error handling techniques provide developers with greater flexibility and control over how errors are managed in PHP applications. These strategies can help you build more robust, maintainable, and user-friendly software by improving error reporting, logging, and recovery mechanisms.

3.4 Performance and Optimization Techniques

Optimizing the performance of your PHP applications is crucial for delivering fast and responsive user experiences. In this section, we'll explore various techniques and best practices for improving the performance of your PHP code.

Code Profiling

Code profiling is the process of analyzing your application's code to identify bottlenecks and performance issues. PHP provides several tools and extensions for profiling, such as Xdebug and XHProf. These tools help you measure execution time, memory usage, and function call counts.

To use Xdebug for profiling, you can add the following configuration to your php.ini file:

[xdebug]

zend_extension=xdebug.so

xdebug.profiler_enable=1

xdebug.profiler_output_dir=/tmp

After configuring Xdebug, you can trigger profiling by adding ?XDEBUG_PROFILE=1 to your application's URL. This generates profiling files that you can analyze to identify performance bottlenecks.

Caching

Caching is a technique that stores frequently accessed data or computed results in memory or files to reduce the need for redundant processing. PHP offers various caching mechanisms:

Opcode Caching

Opcode caching tools like APCu or OPcache store compiled PHP scripts in memory, reducing the need to recompile them on each request. Enabling OPcache in your php.ini file can significantly improve PHP's performance.

[opcache]

zend_extension=opcache.so

opcache.enable=1

opcache.memory_consumption=128

opcache.max_accelerated_files=4000

Data Caching

You can use caching libraries like Memcached or Redis to cache data, such as database query results or rendered HTML. These tools store data in memory, making it quickly accessible without the need for repetitive database queries or expensive computations.

```
$cache = new Memcached();
$cache->addServer("localhost", 11211);
$key = "cached_data_key";
$data = $cache->get($key);
if ($data === false) {
// Data not in cache, fetch and store it
$data = fetchDataFromDatabase();
$cache->set($key, $data, 3600); // Cache for 1 hour
}
// Use the cached data
echo $data;
```

Database Optimization

Optimizing database interactions is crucial for improving application performance. Consider the following strategies:

Indexing

Use appropriate indexes on database columns that are frequently queried. Indexes can significantly speed up SELECT operations.

```
CREATE INDEX idx_username ON users (username);
```

Query Optimization

Write efficient SQL queries, avoiding unnecessary JOINs and selecting only the required columns. Use the EXPLAIN statement to analyze query execution plans and optimize accordingly.

Connection Pooling

Implement a connection pooling mechanism to reuse database connections instead of creating a new connection for each request. Libraries like PDO support connection pooling.

HTTP Caching

Leverage HTTP caching mechanisms to reduce the load on your web server and improve page load times. Set appropriate cache headers in your application to instruct browsers and proxy servers on how to cache resources.

```
// Set cache headers for a resource that rarely changes

header("Cache-Control: max-age=3600"); // Cache for 1 hour
```

Code Optimization

Optimizing your PHP code directly can lead to significant performance gains:

Avoiding Global Variables

Minimize the use of global variables, as they can slow down your code. Instead, use function parameters and return values to pass data between functions.

String Manipulation

When working with strings, use functions like str_replace and strpos instead of regular expressions for simple tasks, as regular expressions can be slower.

Use Compiled Templates

Consider using compiled template engines like Twig or Smarty, which can generate and cache the PHP code for rendering templates. This reduces the need for recompiling templates on each request.

Load Balancing

For high-traffic applications, distribute the load across multiple web servers using load balancing techniques. This ensures that no single server becomes a bottleneck and can handle more concurrent users.

Optimizing PHP application performance is an ongoing process that requires a combination of profiling, caching, database optimization, and code-level improvements. By following these techniques and best practices, you can create PHP applications that deliver faster response times and improved user experiences.

3.5 Security Best Practices in PHP 7

Ensuring the security of your PHP applications is paramount to protect sensitive data, prevent unauthorized access, and safeguard against various threats. In this section, we'll explore security best practices and techniques to fortify your PHP 7 applications.

Input Validation and Sanitization

One of the most critical aspects of security is validating and sanitizing user input. Always validate data received from users or external sources to ensure it conforms to expected formats and constraints. Use functions like filter_var() and regular expressions for validation.

```
$email = $_POST['email'];

if (filter_var($email, FILTER_VALIDATE_EMAIL)) {

// Valid email address

} else {

// Invalid email address

}
```

Additionally, sanitize input to remove any potentially malicious content that could lead to SQL injection, cross-site scripting (XSS), or other vulnerabilities. Utilize functions like mysqli_real_escape_string() when dealing with database queries and prepared statements to prevent SQL injection.

Password Hashing

When storing user passwords, never store them in plain text. Instead, use strong hashing algorithms like bcrypt or Argon2 to hash passwords before saving them in the database. PHP provides the password_hash() and password_verify() functions for secure password handling.

```
$password = $_POST['password'];

// Hash the password before storing it

$hashedPassword = password_hash($password, PASSWORD_BCRYPT);

// Verify the password during login

if (password_verify($password, $hashedPassword)) {

// Password is correct

} else {

// Password is incorrect

}
```

Cross-Site Scripting (XSS) Prevention

Protect your application against XSS attacks by sanitizing and escaping output. Use functions like htmlspecialchars() when displaying user-generated content to ensure that any HTML or JavaScript code within it is treated as plain text.

```
$userInput = $_POST['comment'];

// Display user input while escaping HTML entities
```

```
echo htmlspecialchars($userInput, ENT_QUOTES, 'UTF-8');
```

Cross-Site Request Forgery (CSRF) Protection

Implement CSRF tokens in your forms to prevent attackers from tricking users into making unauthorized actions on your site. Generate unique tokens for each user session and validate them upon form submission.

```
// Generate and store a CSRF token in the user's session

$csrfToken = bin2hex(random_bytes(32));

$_SESSION['csrf_token'] = $csrfToken;

// Include the token in your form

<input type="hidden" name="csrf_token" value="<?= $csrfToken ?>">
```

Session Security

Secure your sessions by setting appropriate session configurations in php.ini, including session cookie settings, session ID regeneration, and session lifetime management. Store sensitive session data in encrypted cookies or a secure database.

File Upload Security

When handling file uploads, ensure that uploaded files are not executable and only contain allowed file types. Limit the upload directory's permissions and validate file types using functions like mime_content_type().

```
$allowedTypes = ['image/jpeg', 'image/png'];

$uploadedFile = $_FILES['file'];
```

```
if (in_array(mime_content_type($uploadedFile['tmp_name']), $allowedTypes)) {

// Process the uploaded file

} else {

// Invalid file type

}
```

Security Headers

Implement security headers in your PHP application to enhance security. Headers like Content Security Policy (CSP), HTTP Strict Transport Security (HSTS), and X-Content-Type-Options can help protect against various attacks.

```
// Enable Content Security Policy

header("Content-Security-Policy: default-src 'self'");

// Enable HTTP Strict Transport Security

header("Strict-Transport-Security: max-age=31536000; includeSubDomains");

// Prevent MIME sniffing

header("X-Content-Type-Options: nosniff");
```

Regular Updates and Patching

Keep your PHP installation, web server, and third-party libraries up to date with the latest security patches. Vulnerabilities in outdated software can be exploited by attackers.

Security Audits and Penetration Testing

Conduct regular security audits and penetration testing to identify and address vulnerabilities in your application. Engage security experts to assess your code and infrastructure for potential weaknesses.

Security is an ongoing process, and it's essential to stay informed about emerging threats and best practices. By following these security best practices in PHP 7, you can significantly reduce the risk of security breaches and protect your application and user data.

Chapter 4: Working with Databases

4.1 Database Connection and Management

Working with databases is a fundamental aspect of many PHP applications. PHP 7 provides robust support for various database systems, including MySQL, PostgreSQL, SQLite, and more. In this section, we'll explore how to establish database connections and manage database interactions using PHP.

Establishing a Database Connection

Before you can interact with a database in PHP, you need to establish a connection to it. This connection allows your PHP scripts to send queries and retrieve data from the database.

MySQL Database Connection

To connect to a MySQL database, you can use the mysqli or PDO (PHP Data Objects) extension. Here's an example using the mysqli extension:

```
$servername = "localhost";

$username = "username";

$password = "password";

$database = "mydb";

// Create a connection

$conn = new mysqli($servername, $username, $password, $database);
```

```
// Check connection
if ($conn->connect_error) {
die("Connection failed: " . $conn->connect_error);
}
```

PDO Database Connection

Using PDO, you can connect to various database types with a consistent API. Here's an example of connecting using PDO:

```
$dsn = "mysql:host=localhost;dbname=mydb";
$username = "username";
$password = "password";
try {
$conn = new PDO($dsn, $username, $password);
$conn->setAttribute(PDO::ATTR_ERRMODE,
PDO::ERRMODE_EXCEPTION);
} catch (PDOException $e) {
die("Connection failed: " . $e->getMessage());
}
```

Executing SQL Queries

Once a database connection is established, you can execute SQL queries to interact with the database. Both mysqli and PDO support executing queries.

Executing Queries with MySQLi

```
$sql = "SELECT * FROM users";
$result = $conn->query($sql);
if ($result->num_rows > 0) {
while ($row = $result->fetch_assoc()) {
echo "ID: " . $row["id"] . " - Name: " . $row["name"] . "<br>";
}
} else {
echo "No records found";
}
$conn->close();
```

Executing Queries with PDO

```
$sql = "SELECT * FROM users";
$stmt = $conn->prepare($sql);
$stmt->execute();
if ($stmt->rowCount() > 0) {
while ($row = $stmt->fetch(PDO::FETCH_ASSOC)) {
echo "ID: " . $row["id"] . " - Name: " . $row["name"] . "<br>";
}
```

```
} else {
echo "No records found";
}
$conn = null;
```

Prepared Statements

Prepared statements are a security best practice when executing SQL queries that involve user input. They prevent SQL injection attacks by separating query logic from user data.

Prepared Statements with MySQLi

```
$sql = "INSERT INTO users (name, email) VALUES (?, ?)";
$stmt = $conn->prepare($sql);
$stmt->bind_param("ss", $name, $email);
$name = "John";
$email = "john@example.com";
$stmt->execute();
echo "Record inserted successfully";
$stmt->close();
$conn->close();
```

Prepared Statements with PDO

```
$sql = "INSERT INTO users (name, email) VALUES (:name, :email)";

$stmt = $conn->prepare($sql);

$name = "Jane";

$email = "jane@example.com";

$stmt->bindParam(":name", $name, PDO::PARAM_STR);

$stmt->bindParam(":email", $email, PDO::PARAM_STR);

$stmt->execute();

echo "Record inserted successfully";

$conn = null;
```

Error Handling in Database Interactions

Proper error handling is essential when working with databases to identify and handle potential issues.

MySQLi Error Handling

```
if ($conn->connect_error) {

die("Connection failed: " . $conn->connect_error);

}

if (!$result) {

die("Query failed: " . $conn->error);
```

```
}
```

PDO Error Handling

```
try {
$conn = new PDO($dsn, $username, $password);
$conn->setAttribute(PDO::ATTR_ERRMODE, PDO::ERRMODE_EXCEPTION);
} catch (PDOException $e) {
die("Connection failed: " . $e->getMessage());
}
if (!$stmt) {
die("Query failed: " . $conn->errorInfo()[2]);
}
```

Working with databases in PHP 7 involves establishing connections, executing queries, using prepared statements for security, and handling errors effectively. These fundamental database management techniques are essential for building robust and reliable PHP applications that interact with data stored in databases.

4.2 Using MySQL with PHP 7

MySQL is one of the most popular relational database management systems, and PHP provides excellent support for connecting, querying, and managing MySQL databases. In this section, we'll explore how to use MySQL with PHP 7.

MySQLi Extension

The MySQL Improved Extension (MySQLi) is a PHP extension specifically designed for working with MySQL databases. It provides both a procedural and an object-oriented API for database interactions.

Procedural Approach

Here's an example of using the MySQLi extension in a procedural manner to connect to a MySQL database and execute queries:

```
$servername = "localhost";

$username = "username";

$password = "password";

$database = "mydb";

// Create a connection

$conn = mysqli_connect($servername, $username, $password, $database);

// Check connection

if (!$conn) {

die("Connection failed: " . mysqli_connect_error());

}

// Execute a SQL query

$sql = "SELECT * FROM users";

$result = mysqli_query($conn, $sql);
```

```
if (mysqli_num_rows($result) > 0) {

while ($row = mysqli_fetch_assoc($result)) {

echo "ID: " . $row["id"] . " - Name: " . $row["name"] . "<br>";

}

} else {

echo "No records found";

}

// Close the connection

mysqli_close($conn);
```

Object-Oriented Approach

Using MySQLi in an object-oriented manner provides a cleaner and more structured way to work with databases:

```
$servername = "localhost";

$username = "username";

$password = "password";

$database = "mydb";

// Create a connection

$conn = new mysqli($servername, $username, $password, $database);

// Check connection
```

```
if ($conn->connect_error) {

die("Connection failed: " . $conn->connect_error);

}

// Execute a SQL query

$sql = "SELECT * FROM users";

$result = $conn->query($sql);

if ($result->num_rows > 0) {

while ($row = $result->fetch_assoc()) {

echo "ID: " . $row["id"] . " - Name: " . $row["name"] . "<br>";

}

} else {

echo "No records found";

}

// Close the connection

$conn->close();
```

PDO Extension

PHP Data Objects (PDO) is another powerful way to work with MySQL databases in PHP. It provides a consistent API for working with various database management systems, including MySQL.

Connecting to MySQL with PDO

Here's an example of connecting to a MySQL database using PDO:

```
$dsn = "mysql:host=localhost;dbname=mydb";

$username = "username";

$password = "password";

try {

$conn = new PDO($dsn, $username, $password);

$conn->setAttribute(PDO::ATTR_ERRMODE, PDO::ERRMODE_EXCEPTION);

} catch (PDOException $e) {

die("Connection failed: " . $e->getMessage());

}
```

Executing Queries with PDO

PDO allows you to execute queries using prepared statements for improved security. Here's an example:

```
$sql = "SELECT * FROM users";

$stmt = $conn->prepare($sql);

$stmt->execute();

if ($stmt->rowCount() > 0) {

while ($row = $stmt->fetch(PDO::FETCH_ASSOC)) {
```

```
echo "ID: " . $row["id"] . " - Name: " . $row["name"] . "<br>";
}
} else {
echo "No records found";
}
```

Choosing Between MySQLi and PDO

Both MySQLi and PDO are robust options for working with MySQL databases in PHP 7. The choice between them often depends on personal preference, project requirements, and coding style. PDO provides a more consistent API for working with different database systems, while MySQLi may offer slightly better performance when working exclusively with MySQL.

In this section, you've learned how to connect to MySQL databases using both MySQLi and PDO extensions in PHP 7, execute queries, and retrieve data. These skills are fundamental for building PHP applications that interact with MySQL databases effectively.

4.3 Advanced SQL Queries and Data Manipulation

In this section, we will delve into advanced SQL queries and data manipulation techniques when working with databases in PHP 7. We'll explore various SQL concepts and how to use them effectively to retrieve, update, and manipulate data within a database.

Joins

SQL JOIN operations allow you to retrieve data from multiple tables based on a related column between them. The most common types of joins are INNER JOIN, LEFT JOIN, RIGHT JOIN, and FULL OUTER JOIN. Here's an example using INNER JOIN to retrieve data from two related tables:

```
SELECT users.name, orders.product

FROM users

INNER JOIN orders ON users.id = orders.user_id;
```

Subqueries

Subqueries, also known as nested queries, allow you to use the result of one query as a part of another query. They are useful for complex data retrieval and manipulation. Here's an example of using a subquery to find users who have placed more than two orders:

```
SELECT name

FROM users

WHERE id IN (

SELECT user_id

FROM orders

GROUP BY user_id

HAVING COUNT(*) > 2

);
```

Transactions

Transactions are essential for ensuring data integrity when performing multiple SQL operations. In PHP, you can use transactions to group a series of SQL statements into a single unit of work that either succeeds entirely or fails entirely. Here's how to use transactions:

```
try {

$conn->beginTransaction();

// Perform multiple SQL operations here

$conn->commit();

} catch (PDOException $e) {

$conn->rollBack();

echo "Transaction failed: " . $e->getMessage();

}
```

Indexing

Database indexing is crucial for optimizing query performance, especially when dealing with large datasets. Indexes provide a quick way to look up data in a table. Common types of indexes include B-tree indexes and full-text indexes. Consider adding indexes to columns frequently used in WHERE clauses or JOIN conditions.

```
CREATE INDEX idx_username ON users (username);
```

Stored Procedures

Stored procedures are precompiled SQL statements that can be executed with a single call. They help improve code reusability and security by encapsulating SQL logic within the database. To create a stored procedure in MySQL, you can use the following syntax:

```
DELIMITER //

CREATE PROCEDURE GetUserInfo(IN userId INT)

BEGIN

SELECT name, email FROM users WHERE id = userId;

END //

DELIMITER ;
```

Triggers

Triggers are database actions that automatically execute in response to specific events, such as INSERT, UPDATE, or DELETE operations on a table. Triggers can be used to enforce business rules, maintain audit logs, or perform other tasks. Here's an example of a simple trigger that logs changes to a user's email:

```
DELIMITER //

CREATE TRIGGER UserEmailChanged

AFTER UPDATE ON users

FOR EACH ROW

BEGIN

INSERT INTO user_logs (user_id, action, timestamp)
```

```
VALUES (NEW.id, 'Email changed', NOW());

END //

DELIMITER ;
```

Views

SQL views are virtual tables created by querying one or more base tables. Views can simplify complex queries, provide data security by restricting access, and enhance data abstraction. To create a view, you can use a SELECT statement:

```
CREATE VIEW active_users AS

SELECT * FROM users WHERE status = 'active';
```

Advanced Data Manipulation

Advanced SQL techniques include working with aggregate functions (e.g., COUNT, SUM, AVG), window functions (e.g., ROW_NUMBER, RANK, DENSE_RANK), and advanced filtering conditions (e.g., GROUP BY, HAVING). These techniques allow you to perform complex data calculations and analyses within the database.

```
SELECT department, AVG(salary) AS avg_salary

FROM employees

GROUP BY department

HAVING AVG(salary) > 50000;
```

Mastering advanced SQL queries and data manipulation techniques in PHP 7 allows you to work effectively with databases, retrieve complex data sets, and optimize query performance. These skills are essential for developing database-driven applications that handle large amounts of data efficiently.

4.4 Using PDO for Database Interactions

In this section, we will focus on using PHP Data Objects (PDO) for database interactions in PHP 7. PDO is a versatile and consistent API that allows you to work with various database management systems, providing a unified approach to database access.

Connecting to a Database with PDO

PDO simplifies the process of connecting to different database systems. To establish a connection, you need to specify the Data Source Name (DSN), username, and password.

```
$dsn = "mysql:host=localhost;dbname=mydb";

$username = "username";

$password = "password";

try {

$conn = new PDO($dsn, $username, $password);

$conn->setAttribute(PDO::ATTR_ERRMODE,
PDO::ERRMODE_EXCEPTION);

} catch (PDOException $e) {

die("Connection failed: " . $e->getMessage());

}
```

Executing SQL Queries

PDO provides a consistent way to execute SQL queries, whether they are SELECT, INSERT, UPDATE, or DELETE statements.

SELECT Query with PDO

```
$sql = "SELECT * FROM users";

$stmt = $conn->query($sql);

if ($stmt->rowCount() > 0) {

while ($row = $stmt->fetch(PDO::FETCH_ASSOC)) {

echo "ID: " . $row["id"] . " - Name: " . $row["name"] . "<br>";

}

} else {

echo "No records found";

}
```

INSERT Query with PDO

```
$sql = "INSERT INTO users (name, email) VALUES (:name, :email)";

$stmt = $conn->prepare($sql);

$name = "John";

$email = "john@example.com";

$stmt->bindParam(":name", $name, PDO::PARAM_STR);
```

```
$stmt->bindParam(":email", $email, PDO::PARAM_STR);

$stmt->execute();

echo "Record inserted successfully";
```

UPDATE Query with PDO

```
$sql = "UPDATE users SET name = :newName WHERE id = :userId";

$stmt = $conn->prepare($sql);

$newName = "Updated Name";

$userId = 1;

$stmt->bindParam(":newName", $newName, PDO::PARAM_STR);

$stmt->bindParam(":userId", $userId, PDO::PARAM_INT);

$stmt->execute();

echo "Record updated successfully";
```

DELETE Query with PDO

```
$sql = "DELETE FROM users WHERE id = :userId";

$stmt = $conn->prepare($sql);

$userId = 2;

$stmt->bindParam(":userId", $userId, PDO::PARAM_INT);

$stmt->execute();
```

```
echo "Record deleted successfully";
```

Prepared Statements

PDO encourages the use of prepared statements for executing SQL queries. Prepared statements provide security by separating SQL logic from user data, preventing SQL injection.

```
$sql = "SELECT * FROM users WHERE id = :userId";

$stmt = $conn->prepare($sql);

$userId = 1;

$stmt->bindParam(":userId", $userId, PDO::PARAM_INT);

$stmt->execute();

if ($stmt->rowCount() > 0) {

$row = $stmt->fetch(PDO::FETCH_ASSOC);

echo "ID: " . $row["id"] . " - Name: " . $row["name"];

} else {

echo "No record found";

}
```

Error Handling

PDO makes it easy to handle database errors using exceptions. You can catch exceptions and handle errors gracefully.

```
try {

// Database operations here
```

```
} catch (PDOException $e) {

echo "Database error: " . $e->getMessage();

}
```

Transactions with PDO

PDO supports transactions, allowing you to group multiple database operations into a single unit of work. Transactions ensure that all operations either succeed or fail together.

```
try {

$conn->beginTransaction();

// Database operations

$conn->commit();

} catch (PDOException $e) {

$conn->rollBack();

echo "Transaction failed: " . $e->getMessage();

}
```

Fetching Data

PDO provides various fetch methods to retrieve data in different formats, such as associative arrays, objects, or both.

```
// Fetch as associative array

$row = $stmt->fetch(PDO::FETCH_ASSOC);

// Fetch as object
```

```
$row = $stmt->fetch(PDO::FETCH_OBJ);

// Fetch all rows as associative arrays

$rows = $stmt->fetchAll(PDO::FETCH_ASSOC);
```

PHP Data Objects (PDO) is a versatile and powerful tool for working with databases in PHP 7. Its unified API allows you to connect to various database systems and perform database operations with consistency and security. Whether you need to execute queries, use prepared statements, handle transactions, or fetch data, PDO provides a robust solution for database interactions in PHP.

4.5 Securing Database Transactions

Securing database transactions is of utmost importance when developing PHP applications that interact with databases. In this section, we will explore best practices and techniques to enhance the security of your database transactions in PHP 7.

Prepared Statements for Security

One of the fundamental security practices when working with databases is the use of prepared statements. Prepared statements separate SQL code from user input, effectively preventing SQL injection attacks. By binding parameters to placeholders in your SQL queries, you ensure that user data is treated as data rather than executable code.

```
// Using prepared statements with PDO

$sql = "SELECT * FROM users WHERE username = :username AND password = :password";
```

```
$stmt = $conn->prepare($sql);

$username = $_POST["username"];

$password = $_POST["password"];

$stmt->bindParam(":username", $username, PDO::PARAM_STR);

$stmt->bindParam(":password", $password, PDO::PARAM_STR);

$stmt->execute();
```

Input Validation

Input validation is crucial to ensure that the data submitted to your application is valid and safe to use. Even with prepared statements, validating user input can help prevent potential issues. PHP provides filter functions for this purpose, such as filter_var() and filter_input().

```
$username = $_POST["username"];

if (filter_var($username, FILTER_VALIDATE_EMAIL)) {

// Valid email address

} else {

// Invalid email address

}
```

Password Hashing

Storing passwords securely is essential to protect user data. PHP provides functions like password_hash() and password_verify() for secure password hashing and verification. Never store plain text passwords in your database.

```
$password = $_POST["password"];

// Hash the password before storing it

$hashedPassword = password_hash($password, PASSWORD_DEFAULT);
```

User Authentication

Implementing proper user authentication is a critical aspect of database security. Verify user credentials securely before granting access to sensitive data or actions.

```
$username = $_POST["username"];

$password = $_POST["password"];

$sql = "SELECT * FROM users WHERE username = :username";

$stmt = $conn->prepare($sql);

$stmt->bindParam(":username", $username, PDO::PARAM_STR);

$stmt->execute();

if ($stmt->rowCount() > 0) {

$row = $stmt->fetch(PDO::FETCH_ASSOC);

if (password_verify($password, $row["password"])) {

// Authentication successful

} else {
```

```
// Authentication failed
}
} else {
// User not found
}
```

Proper Authorization

In addition to authentication, ensure proper authorization to restrict access to specific resources or actions. Only authorized users should be allowed to perform certain database transactions.

```
// Check if the user has the necessary permissions
if ($userRole === "admin") {
// Perform admin-specific database operations
} else {
// Unauthorized access
}
```

SQL Injection Prevention

Always validate and sanitize user input to prevent SQL injection attacks. Avoid constructing SQL queries by concatenating user input directly. Use prepared statements, as shown earlier, to eliminate the risk of SQL injection.

Error Handling

Implement comprehensive error handling for your database transactions. Catch and log database errors to help identify and address issues promptly. Avoid exposing sensitive information in error messages that could be exploited by attackers.

```
try {
// Database operations here
} catch (PDOException $e) {
// Log the error and handle it gracefully
error_log("Database error: " . $e->getMessage());
}
```

Regular Updates and Patching

Keep your PHP version, database server, and related software up to date with security patches. Regular updates help protect your application from known vulnerabilities.

Data Encryption

Consider encrypting sensitive data, both in transit and at rest. Use HTTPS for secure data transmission, and encrypt sensitive information before storing it in the database.

Securing database transactions is an ongoing process that requires attention to detail and adherence to best practices. By implementing these security measures and staying informed about the latest security threats and solutions, you can significantly enhance the security of your PHP 7 applications that interact with databases.

Chapter 5: Web Development with PHP 7

5.1 Building Dynamic Web Pages

Web development with PHP 7 opens up endless possibilities for creating dynamic and interactive web applications. In this section, we'll explore the fundamentals of building dynamic web pages using PHP 7 and how PHP can be integrated with HTML to create web applications that respond to user input and deliver dynamic content.

Mixing PHP and HTML

One of the strengths of PHP is its ability to seamlessly integrate with HTML. You can embed PHP code directly within your HTML pages, allowing you to generate dynamic content and respond to user actions.

```
<!DOCTYPE html>

<html>

<head>

<title>Dynamic Web Page</title>

</head>

<body>

<h1>Welcome, <?php echo "John Doe"; ?></h1>

<p>Today's date is <?php echo date("Y-m-d"); ?></p>

</body>
```

```
</html>
```

In the example above, PHP code within <?php ?> tags is used to dynamically generate content. You can include variables, functions, and control structures to customize the HTML output based on data from your PHP script.

Handling Form Submissions

Web applications often require user input and interaction. PHP is well-suited for processing form submissions, allowing users to input data and interact with your application.

```
<form method="post" action="process.php">

<label for="name">Name:</label>

<input type="text" id="name" name="name">

<input type="submit" value="Submit">

</form>
```

In the example above, a simple HTML form is created. When the user submits the form, the data is sent to a PHP script specified in the action attribute. PHP can then process the form data, validate it, and take appropriate actions.

Server-Side Processing

PHP enables server-side processing, which means that logic and data manipulation occur on the server before delivering the final HTML to the client's browser. This allows you to perform tasks like database queries, file handling, and authentication securely on the server.

```
// PHP script for processing form data
```

```
if ($_SERVER["REQUEST_METHOD"] === "POST") {

$name = $_POST["name"];

echo "Hello, $name!";

}
```

In the PHP script above, the server receives the form data, processes it, and sends a personalized response to the client's browser. Server-side processing is crucial for security and data integrity.

Building Dynamic Content

PHP allows you to build web pages with dynamic content that can change based on various factors such as user input, database queries, or external data sources.

```
<ul>

<?php

// Generate a dynamic list from an array

$items = ["Item 1", "Item 2", "Item 3"];

foreach ($items as $item) {

echo "<li>$item</li>";

}

?>

</ul>
```

In this example, PHP is used to generate an HTML list dynamically based on an array. This can be particularly useful for displaying data retrieved from a database or any situation where content needs to be generated on the fly.

Session Management

Web applications often require session management to maintain user state across multiple requests. PHP provides built-in support for session handling, allowing you to store and retrieve session data securely.

```
// Starting a session

session_start();

// Storing data in a session

$_SESSION["user_id"] = 123;

// Retrieving session data

$user_id = $_SESSION["user_id"];
```

Using PHP sessions, you can create personalized user experiences, implement authentication mechanisms, and track user activity on your web application.

Templating Engines

While embedding PHP code within HTML is a common practice, larger and more complex web applications may benefit from using templating engines such as Twig or Smarty. These engines separate the presentation layer from the business logic, making it easier to manage and maintain your codebase.

Security Considerations

When building dynamic web pages with PHP, it's essential to consider security. Always validate and sanitize user input to prevent malicious input and SQL injection attacks. Implement proper authentication and authorization mechanisms to protect sensitive data and actions.

Conclusion

Building dynamic web pages with PHP 7 is a powerful way to create interactive and engaging web applications. By integrating PHP seamlessly with HTML, handling form submissions, performing server-side processing, and managing sessions, you can develop web applications that respond to user input and deliver dynamic content. Stay mindful of security best practices to ensure the safety of your web application and its users.

5.2 Managing User Sessions and Cookies

User sessions and cookies are fundamental concepts in web development when it comes to maintaining user state and personalization. In this section, we will explore how PHP 7 can be used to manage user sessions and cookies effectively.

Understanding User Sessions

A session is a way to persist user data across multiple requests. PHP manages sessions through a unique session ID stored as a cookie or in the URL. By default, PHP stores session data on the server, making it a secure way to maintain user state.

To start a session in PHP, use the session_start() function. This function should be called before any output is sent to the browser.

```
<?php

session_start();

?>
```

Storing Data in Sessions

You can store user-specific data in sessions, making it accessible across multiple pages of your website. For example, you can store a user's login status, username, or other relevant information.

```
<?php

// Storing data in a session

$_SESSION["username"] = "john_doe";

?>
```

The data stored in the session will be available throughout the user's visit until the session is destroyed or expires.

Retrieving Data from Sessions

Retrieving data from sessions is straightforward. Use the $_SESSION superglobal array to access session variables.

```
<?php

// Retrieving data from a session

$username = $_SESSION["username"];

?>
```

You can retrieve and display user-specific information based on their session data, providing personalized experiences.

Session Variables Lifetime

By default, session variables exist as long as the user's browser is open. When the browser is closed, the session typically ends, and the session data is deleted. However, you can set session variables to last longer by modifying the session configuration.

```
<?php

// Set the session cookie to expire in one hour

ini_set('session.cookie_lifetime', 3600);

?>
```

Handling Cookies

Cookies are small pieces of data stored on the user's device. PHP can set and retrieve cookies to remember user preferences, login status, or other data. Cookies can have an expiration date, making them persistent across browser sessions.

Setting Cookies

You can use the setcookie() function to set cookies in PHP.

```
<?php

// Setting a cookie that expires in 7 days

setcookie("username", "john_doe", time() + 7 * 24 * 3600);

?>
```

The above code sets a cookie named "username" with the value "john_doe" and an expiration time of 7 days from the current time.

Retrieving Cookies

To retrieve cookies, you can use the $_COOKIE superglobal.

```
<?php
// Retrieving a cookie
$username = $_COOKIE["username"];
?>
```

Security Considerations

When dealing with user sessions and cookies, security is paramount. Always validate and sanitize user input, especially when dealing with cookies, to prevent potential security vulnerabilities.

For session management, use secure and random session IDs, and consider implementing session fixation and session hijacking prevention techniques. Additionally, sanitize and validate data stored in cookies to avoid security risks.

Conclusion

Managing user sessions and cookies is crucial for building interactive and personalized web applications. PHP 7 provides robust tools for handling sessions and setting/retrieving cookies, allowing you to create dynamic and user-friendly websites. Be mindful of security best practices to protect sensitive data and ensure a safe browsing experience for your users.

5.3 Form Handling and Data Validation

Form handling and data validation are essential aspects of web development with PHP 7. In this section, we will explore how PHP can be used to process forms submitted by users and ensure that the data is validated and sanitized for security and accuracy.

Creating HTML Forms

HTML forms are used to collect user data, such as user registration, login, search queries, or feedback submission. To create a form in HTML, you use the <form> element along with various input elements like text fields, radio buttons, checkboxes, and buttons.

```
<form method="post" action="process.php">

<label for="name">Name:</label>

<input type="text" id="name" name="name">

<br>

<label for="email">Email:</label>

<input type="email" id="email" name="email">

<br>

<input type="submit" value="Submit">

</form>
```

In the above example, we have a simple HTML form with input fields for the user's name and email. The form's action attribute specifies the URL to which the form data will be sent for processing.

Processing Form Data

Once a user submits a form, PHP can handle the submitted data. The form data is sent to a PHP script specified in the form's action attribute. The PHP script can access the form data through the $_POST or $_GET superglobal arrays, depending on the form's method attribute.

```
<?php
if ($_SERVER["REQUEST_METHOD"] === "POST") {
$name = $_POST["name"];
$email = $_POST["email"];
// Process the data, perform validation, and save to the database
}
?>
```

Data Validation

Data validation is crucial to ensure that the submitted data is accurate and safe to use. PHP provides various functions and filters for validating user input.

For example, you can use the filter_var() function to validate an email address:

```
$email = $_POST["email"];
if (filter_var($email, FILTER_VALIDATE_EMAIL)) {
// Valid email address
} else {
```

```
// Invalid email address
}
```

You can also validate other types of data, such as integers or URLs, using appropriate filter flags.

Sanitization

Sanitization is the process of cleaning and filtering user input to remove any potentially harmful or unwanted characters. This helps prevent security vulnerabilities, such as SQL injection or Cross-Site Scripting (XSS) attacks.

PHP offers functions like filter_var() with different filter flags for sanitizing data. For example, to sanitize a string and remove any HTML tags, you can use:

```
$userInput = $_POST["user_input"];
$cleanedInput = filter_var($userInput, FILTER_SANITIZE_STRING);
```

Error Handling

Effective error handling is essential when processing form data. If validation fails or an error occurs during data processing, it's crucial to provide clear and user-friendly error messages to guide users.

```
$errors = [];
if (empty($name)) {
$errors[] = "Name is required";
}
```

```
if (!filter_var($email, FILTER_VALIDATE_EMAIL)) {
$errors[] = "Invalid email address";
}
if (empty($errors)) {
// Process the data and save it to the database
} else {
// Display error messages to the user
foreach ($errors as $error) {
echo "<p>$error</p>";
}
}
```

CAPTCHA and Anti-Spam Measures

To prevent automated spam submissions, you can implement CAPTCHA (Completely Automated Public Turing test to tell Computers and Humans Apart) or other anti-spam measures in your forms. Several libraries and services are available for integrating CAPTCHA into your PHP forms.

Conclusion

Form handling and data validation are integral parts of web development with PHP 7. By creating HTML forms, processing submitted data, validating input, and implementing error handling, you can build robust and secure web applications that collect and utilize user data effectively. Ensuring data accuracy and security is essential for providing a positive user experience and protecting your application from potential vulnerabilities.

5.4 File Uploads and Handling

File uploads are a common requirement in web applications, allowing users to share images, documents, and other files. In this section, we will explore how to handle file uploads in PHP 7 and perform various tasks such as validation, storage, and security measures.

HTML File Upload Form

To allow users to upload files, you need an HTML form with an <input> element of type file. Here's a simple example of an HTML file upload form:

```
<form action="upload.php" method="post" enctype="multipart/form-data">

<input type="file" name="fileToUpload" id="fileToUpload">

<input type="submit" value="Upload File" name="submit">

</form>
```

The enctype="multipart/form-data" attribute is crucial when handling file uploads, as it specifies that the form data includes binary file data.

PHP File Upload Handling

In PHP, you can access uploaded files through the $_FILES superglobal array. When a user submits the form, PHP populates this array with information about the uploaded file.

```
if ($_SERVER["REQUEST_METHOD"] === "POST") {

$file = $_FILES["fileToUpload"];

$fileName = $file["name"];

$fileSize = $file["size"];

$fileType = $file["type"];

$fileTmpName = $file["tmp_name"];

// Perform file handling operations

}
```

File Validation

Before processing an uploaded file, it's essential to validate it to ensure it meets your application's requirements. Common validations include checking the file type, size, and ensuring it does not contain any security threats.

```
$allowedTypes = ["image/jpeg", "image/png", "application/pdf"];

$maxFileSize = 5 * 1024 * 1024; // 5 MB

if (!in_array($fileType, $allowedTypes)) {

// Invalid file type

}

if ($fileSize > $maxFileSize) {

// File size exceeds the allowed limit

}
```

Secure File Handling

Security is paramount when dealing with file uploads. To prevent security vulnerabilities like arbitrary code execution, it's crucial to store uploaded files in a secure location and ensure they cannot be executed as scripts.

One common approach is to store uploaded files outside of the web root directory, so they cannot be accessed directly via a URL. Additionally, you can rename uploaded files to avoid conflicts and ensure unique filenames.

```
$uploadDirectory = "/path/to/upload/directory/";

$newFileName = uniqid() . "_" . $fileName;

$targetPath = $uploadDirectory . $newFileName;

if (move_uploaded_file($fileTmpName, $targetPath)) {

// File uploaded successfully

} else {

// Error occurred during file upload

}
```

File Upload Progress

For large file uploads, you may want to provide users with feedback on the upload progress. PHP's $_FILES array provides information about the upload progress, including the $_FILES['file']['size'] and $_FILES['file']['bytes_processed'] values.

Handling Multiple Files

To handle multiple file uploads in a single form, you can use array notation in the HTML input field's name attribute and iterate through the $_FILES array.

```
<form action="upload.php" method="post" enctype="multipart/form-data">

<input type="file" name="filesToUpload[]" multiple>

<input type="submit" value="Upload Files" name="submit">

</form>

if ($_SERVER["REQUEST_METHOD"] === "POST") {

$files = $_FILES["filesToUpload"];

foreach ($files["tmp_name"] as $index => $fileTmpName) {

$fileName = $files["name"][$index];

// Process each uploaded file

}

}
```

Conclusion

File uploads and handling are essential features in many web applications. With PHP 7, you can create secure and efficient file upload systems that allow users to share files while ensuring data integrity and security. Implementing validation, secure storage, and other security measures is crucial to providing a safe and reliable file upload experience for both users and the application.

5.5 Creating RESTful APIs with PHP 7

Representational State Transfer (REST) is an architectural style for designing networked applications. RESTful APIs (Application Programming Interfaces) are a common way to expose the functionality of web applications, allowing other applications to interact with them over HTTP. In this section, we will explore how to create RESTful APIs using PHP 7, enabling communication between different software systems.

Understanding RESTful APIs

RESTful APIs adhere to the principles of REST, which include using HTTP methods (GET, POST, PUT, DELETE) to perform actions on resources identified by URLs. These APIs use a stateless client-server architecture, meaning that each request from a client to a server must contain all the information needed to understand and fulfill the request.

Building RESTful Endpoints

To create a RESTful API in PHP, you need to define endpoints, which are URLs that represent specific resources or actions. For example, a simple RESTful API for managing books might have endpoints like:

- /api/books to get a list of all books
- /api/books/{id} to get details of a specific book by its ID
- /api/books with a POST request to create a new book
- /api/books/{id} with a PUT request to update a book

- /api/books/{id} with a DELETE request to delete a book

Handling HTTP Requests

In PHP, you can handle different HTTP methods and their associated actions using conditional statements. For example, you can use $_SERVER['REQUEST_METHOD'] to determine the HTTP method used in the request and then perform the corresponding action.

```
if ($_SERVER['REQUEST_METHOD'] === 'GET') {

// Handle GET request

} elseif ($_SERVER['REQUEST_METHOD'] === 'POST') {

// Handle POST request

} elseif ($_SERVER['REQUEST_METHOD'] === 'PUT') {

// Handle PUT request

} elseif ($_SERVER['REQUEST_METHOD'] === 'DELETE') {

// Handle DELETE request

} else {

// Handle unsupported methods

}
```

Sending and Receiving JSON Data

RESTful APIs commonly use JSON (JavaScript Object Notation) as the data format for communication. PHP provides functions for encoding and decoding JSON data.

To send JSON responses, you can use json_encode():

```
$data = ['message' => 'Hello, World!'];

echo json_encode($data);
```

To receive and parse JSON data in the request body, you can use json_decode():

```
$jsonData = file_get_contents('php://input');

$data = json_decode($jsonData, true);
```

Implementing Authentication and Authorization

RESTful APIs often require authentication and authorization to ensure that only authorized users or applications can access certain endpoints. You can implement authentication using techniques like API keys, OAuth, or token-based authentication.

For example, you can use JWT (JSON Web Tokens) for token-based authentication in PHP.

Handling Errors

In RESTful APIs, it's essential to provide meaningful error responses to clients when something goes wrong. You can use HTTP status codes to indicate the outcome of a request:

- 200 OK for successful requests
- 201 Created for successful resource creation
- 204 No Content for successful request with no response body
- 400 Bad Request for client errors (e.g., invalid input)

- 401 Unauthorized for authentication failures
- 404 Not Found for resources that don't exist
- 500 Internal Server Error for server errors

Rate Limiting and Throttling

To prevent abuse of your API, you may want to implement rate limiting and request throttling. These mechanisms limit the number of requests a client can make within a specific time frame.

Documentation and Versioning

Proper documentation of your API is crucial to help developers understand how to use it. Additionally, consider versioning your API to ensure backward compatibility while allowing for future enhancements.

Conclusion

Creating RESTful APIs with PHP 7 allows you to expose your application's functionality to other systems and developers. By adhering to REST principles, defining clear endpoints, handling HTTP requests, using JSON for data exchange, implementing authentication and authorization, and providing error handling and documentation, you can build robust and interoperable APIs that facilitate communication between different software components and services.

Chapter 6: PHP 7 Frameworks and Libraries

Section 6.1: Introduction to Popular PHP Frameworks

In this section, we will delve into the exciting world of PHP frameworks. PHP frameworks are pre-built software packages that provide a structured foundation for building web applications. They offer a set of tools, libraries, and best practices that streamline the development process, improve code organization, and enhance maintainability. PHP frameworks have gained immense popularity in recent years due to their ability to simplify and accelerate web application development.

Why Use a PHP Framework?

Before we explore specific PHP frameworks, it's important to understand the advantages they offer:

1. **Rapid Development**: PHP frameworks provide pre-built modules and libraries that save developers from reinventing the wheel. This accelerates development and reduces the time-to-market for your web applications.
2. **Code Organization**: Frameworks enforce a structured coding approach, making it easier to organize your codebase. This enhances maintainability and collaboration among developers.
3. **Security**: Most PHP frameworks come with built-in security features, such as protection against common web vulnerabilities like SQL injection and cross-site scripting (XSS) attacks.
4. **Scalability**: Frameworks are designed with scalability in mind, allowing your application to grow seamlessly as

traffic increases.

5. **Community Support**: PHP frameworks often have active communities, which means you can find a wealth of documentation, tutorials, and plugins to extend functionality.

Now, let's explore some of the most popular PHP frameworks:

Laravel

Laravel is a modern and elegant PHP framework known for its developer-friendly syntax and robust features. It follows the Model-View-Controller (MVC) architectural pattern, making it easy to separate concerns in your application. Laravel includes features like an expressive ORM (Eloquent), a powerful routing system, authentication, and Blade templating.

Example of a Laravel route definition:

```
Route::get('/dashboard', 'DashboardController@index');
```

Symfony

Symfony is a highly flexible and extensible PHP framework that is often used for large-scale applications. It provides reusable components (Symfony Components) that can be integrated into your project as needed. Symfony emphasizes best practices and adheres to the PSR standards, ensuring code quality.

Example of creating a Symfony controller:

```
use Symfony\Bundle\FrameworkBundle\Controller\AbstractController;
```

```
use Symfony\Component\HttpFoundation\Response;

class HomeController extends AbstractController

{

public function index(): Response

{

return $this->render('home/index.html.twig', [

'controller_name' => 'HomeController',

]);

}

}
```

CodeIgniter

CodeIgniter is a lightweight and straightforward PHP framework that's ideal for small to medium-sized projects. It offers excellent performance and a small footprint. CodeIgniter doesn't force a specific coding structure on developers, giving you the freedom to design your application as you see fit.

Example of a CodeIgniter controller:

```
class Blog extends CI_Controller {

public function index()

{

$this->load->view('blog');
```

```
}
}
```

Yii

Yii is a high-performance PHP framework suitable for developing web 2.0 applications. It incorporates features like database abstraction, caching, and role-based access control. Yii's strong command-line tools enable developers to generate code and scaffolding quickly.

Example of defining a Yii controller action:

```php
public function actionView($id)
{
$model = Post::findOne($id);
return $this->render('view', [
'model' => $model,
]);
}
```

These are just a few examples of popular PHP frameworks, each with its unique strengths and use cases. As you continue your journey into PHP web development, you'll have the opportunity to explore these frameworks and choose the one that best suits your project's requirements.

Section 6.2: Building Applications with Laravel

Laravel is a powerful and elegant PHP framework that has gained significant popularity in the web development community. In this section, we will explore building web applications with Laravel and understand why it's widely acclaimed.

Getting Started with Laravel

To start using Laravel for your web development projects, you first need to install it. The most common way to do this is by using Composer, a PHP dependency manager. You can create a new Laravel project by running the following command:

composer create-project—prefer-dist laravel/laravel mylaravelapp

This command fetches the latest Laravel version and sets up a new project in a directory called mylaravelapp. Once the installation is complete, you can navigate to the project directory and start building your application.

The MVC Architecture

Laravel follows the Model-View-Controller (MVC) architectural pattern, which is a proven way to organize code and separate concerns in your application.

- **Model**: Models represent the data structures and the business logic of your application. In Laravel, models are typically stored in the app/Models directory. You can create a new model using Artisan, Laravel's command-line tool.

  php artisan make:model Post

- **View**: Views are responsible for displaying data to the user. In Laravel, views are stored in the resources/views directory. You can use Blade, Laravel's templating engine, to create dynamic and reusable templates.

Example Blade template:

```
<h1>Welcome, {{ $user->name }}</h1>
```

- **Controller**: Controllers handle the incoming HTTP requests, process them, and interact with models and views. Controllers in Laravel are stored in the app/Http/Controllers directory. You can create a new controller using Artisan as well.

```
php artisan make:controller PostController
```

Routing

Laravel provides a powerful routing system that allows you to define how incoming HTTP requests should be handled. Routes are defined in the routes/web.php file.

Example of a basic route definition:

```
Route::get('/about', function () {

return view('about');

});
```

In this example, when a user visits the /about URL, Laravel will execute the anonymous function and return the about view.

Database Interaction

Laravel's Eloquent ORM makes working with databases a breeze. You can define your database schema using migrations and interact with your database tables using Eloquent models.

Example migration to create a posts table:

```
php artisan make:migration create_posts_table
```

After defining the schema in the migration file, you can run the migration to create the table:

```
php artisan migrate
```

Creating a corresponding Eloquent model:

```
php artisan make:model Post
```

Now you can perform database operations like creating, updating, and querying records using the Post model.

```
// Create a new post

$post = new Post;

$post->title = 'New Post';

$post->content = 'This is the content of the post.';

$post->save();

// Retrieve posts

$posts = Post::all();

// Update a post

$post = Post::find(1);
```

```
$post->title = 'Updated Post';

$post->save();
```

Authentication and Authorization

Laravel comes with built-in authentication and authorization features, making it easy to implement user registration, login, and access control.

To scaffold the authentication system, you can use Artisan:

```
php artisan make:auth
```

This command generates the necessary views, controllers, and routes for user registration and authentication.

Conclusion

Laravel is a versatile and feature-rich PHP framework that simplifies web application development. In this section, we've scratched the surface of what Laravel can do. As you explore further, you'll discover its extensive ecosystem of packages, libraries, and tools that can help you build robust and scalable web applications with ease.

Section 6.3: Web Development with Symfony

Symfony is a powerful PHP framework known for its flexibility, scalability, and adherence to best practices. In this section, we will delve into web development with Symfony and explore its core concepts and features.

Getting Started with Symfony

To begin using Symfony for your web development projects, you'll need to install it. The recommended way to set up a new Symfony project is by using Symfony's official installer, Symfony CLI. You can create a new Symfony project by running the following command:

symfony new my_symfony_project

This command will fetch the latest Symfony version and set up a new project in a directory called my_symfony_project. After installation, you can navigate to the project directory and start building your Symfony application.

Symfony's Architecture

Symfony follows the Model-View-Controller (MVC) architectural pattern, which encourages a clean separation of concerns in your application.

- **Model**: In Symfony, models represent the data structures and interact with the database. Doctrine, a powerful Object-Relational Mapping (ORM) tool, is commonly used with Symfony for database operations. You can define your entities and their relationships using Doctrine annotations.

```
/**
* @Entity
* @Table(name="products")
*/
```

```
class Product

{

/**

* @Id

* @GeneratedValue(strategy="AUTO")

* @Column(type="integer")

*/

protected $id;

// Other properties and methods

}
```

- **View**: Views in Symfony are responsible for rendering the output. Symfony uses the Twig templating engine by default, allowing you to create dynamic and reusable templates.

Example Twig template:

```
<h1>Welcome, {{ user.name }}</h1>
```

- **Controller**: Controllers handle incoming HTTP requests, process them, and interact with models and views. Controllers in Symfony are PHP classes that are responsible for handling specific routes and actions.

Example Symfony controller action:

```
public function index()
{
return $this->render('product/index.html.twig', [
'products' => $products,
]);
}
```

Routing

Symfony provides a robust routing system that allows you to define how incoming HTTP requests should be handled. Routes are typically configured in the config/routes.yaml file.

Example of a basic route definition:

```
product_list:
path: /products
controller: App\Controller\ProductController::index
```

In this example, when a user visits the /products URL, Symfony will invoke the index action in the ProductController.

Database Interaction with Doctrine

Doctrine is a powerful ORM tool that simplifies database interactions in Symfony. You can define your database schema using Doctrine annotations or XML/YAML configuration files.

Example of a Doctrine entity definition with annotations:

```
/**
* @Entity
* @Table(name="products")
*/
class Product
{
/**
* @Id
* @GeneratedValue(strategy="AUTO")
* @Column(type="integer")
*/
protected $id;
/**
* @Column(type="string")
*/
protected $name;
// Other properties and methods
}
```

After defining your entities, you can use Doctrine's command-line tools to generate database tables and perform migrations.

Twig Templating

Twig is Symfony's default templating engine, known for its simplicity and readability. Twig templates allow you to create dynamic and structured views for your application.

Example Twig template:

```
<h1>Product List</h1>

<ul>

{% for product in products %}

<li>{{ product.name }}</li>

{% endfor %}

</ul>
```

Twig provides features like template inheritance, filters, and functions, making it a powerful tool for building your application's views.

Conclusion

Symfony is a versatile PHP framework that offers a robust set of tools for web development. In this section, we've explored some of its core concepts, including its architecture, routing system, database interaction with Doctrine, and Twig templating. Symfony's strong community support and adherence to best practices make it a solid choice for building complex web applications that require scalability and maintainability. As you dive deeper into Symfony, you'll discover its extensive documentation and ecosystem of bundles and components that can streamline your development process further.

Section 6.4: Using Composer for Dependency Management

Composer is a powerful tool for managing dependencies in PHP projects, and it plays a crucial role in the Symfony ecosystem. In this section, we'll explore how Composer works and how you can use it effectively in your Symfony projects.

Understanding Composer

Composer is a dependency management tool for PHP that allows you to declare and manage project dependencies. It simplifies the process of including external libraries and packages into your project. Symfony and many other PHP frameworks and libraries rely on Composer for package management.

Installing Composer

To use Composer, you need to install it globally on your system. You can download the Composer installer script and execute it using the following command:

```
php -r "copy('https://getcomposer.org/installer', 'composer-setup.php');"

php -r "if (hash_file('sha384', 'composer-setup.php') === 'YOUR_HASH_HERE') { echo 'Installer verified'; } else { echo 'Installer corrupt'; unlink('composer-setup.php'); } echo PHP_EOL;"

php composer-setup.php

php -r "unlink('composer-setup.php');"

sudo mv composer.phar /usr/local/bin/composer
```

Replace YOUR_HASH_HERE with the actual hash shown on the Composer website for the latest installer.

Creating a Symfony Project with Composer

Composer is commonly used to create new Symfony projects. You can create a new Symfony project using the Symfony CLI tool and Composer. Here's the command to create a new Symfony project:

```
symfony new my_symfony_project
```

This command uses Composer to fetch the required Symfony packages and set up a new Symfony project.

Managing Dependencies

Once you have a Symfony project, you can manage its dependencies using the composer.json file. This file lists all the required packages and their versions. You can add new dependencies to your project by editing this file or by using Composer's command-line tools.

To add a new dependency, you can run the following Composer command:

```
composer require vendor/package-name
```

Composer will fetch the package and update the composer.json file with the new requirement.

Autoloading with Composer

Composer simplifies class autoloading by generating an autoloader file for your project. This autoloader allows you to use classes and functions from your project's dependencies without manually including each file.

Symfony and many PHP packages follow the PSR-4 autoloading standard. Composer generates an autoloader that adheres to this standard, making it easy to autoload classes from various packages.

```
// Autoload Composer's generated autoloader

require 'vendor/autoload.php';

// Now you can use classes from your project's dependencies

use Symfony\Component\HttpFoundation\Request;
```

Composer Scripts

Composer allows you to define custom scripts in your composer.json file, enabling you to automate various tasks within your Symfony project. These scripts can include tasks like database migrations, asset compilation, and more.

```
{

"scripts": {

"post-install-cmd": [

"php bin/console doctrine:migrations:migrate"

],

"post-update-cmd": [

"php bin/console doctrine:schema:update—force"

]

}

}
```

In this example, Composer will execute the specified Symfony console commands automatically after installing or updating packages.

Conclusion

Composer is a fundamental tool for managing dependencies in Symfony and other PHP projects. It simplifies the process of including external libraries and packages, streamlining your development workflow. Understanding how to use Composer effectively is essential for Symfony developers, as it allows you to leverage Symfony's extensive ecosystem of packages and components to build robust web applications.

Section 6.5: Unit Testing with PHPUnit

Unit testing is an essential practice in modern software development that helps ensure the correctness of your code. In Symfony, you can use PHPUnit, a widely adopted testing framework for PHP, to write and execute unit tests for your Symfony applications. In this section, we'll explore how to perform unit testing with PHPUnit in Symfony.

Setting Up PHPUnit

Before you can start writing unit tests, you need to ensure PHPUnit is installed in your Symfony project. Typically, PHPUnit is included as a development dependency using Composer. You can add it to your project like this:

composer require—dev phpunit/phpunit

Once PHPUnit is installed, you can configure your test suite. Symfony projects often come with a phpunit.xml.dist file that contains configuration settings for PHPUnit.

Writing Unit Tests

Symfony follows the PSR-4 autoloading standard, making it easy to write and organize unit tests. By convention, unit tests for Symfony applications are stored in a directory called tests within your project's root directory.

You can create a unit test class for a Symfony component or service using the following naming convention: <ServiceName>Test. For example, if you want to test a service called UserService, the corresponding test class would be named UserServiceTest.

Here's a basic example of a unit test for a Symfony service using PHPUnit:

```
use PHPUnit\Framework\TestCase;

use App\Service\UserService;

class UserServiceTest extends TestCase

{

public function testCreateUser()

{

// Arrange

$userService = new UserService();

// Act

$user = $userService->createUser('John Doe', 'johndoe@example.com');

// Assert
```

```
$this->assertInstanceOf(User::class, $user);

$this->assertEquals('John Doe', $user->getName());

$this->assertEquals('johndoe@example.com', $user->getEmail());

}

}
```

In this example, we've created a unit test for the UserService class's createUser method. The test asserts that the method returns a User object with the expected properties.

Running Unit Tests

To execute your unit tests, you can use PHPUnit's command-line interface. By default, PHPUnit looks for test files in the tests directory and files with names ending in Test.php. You can run your tests using the following command:

```
./vendor/bin/phpunit
```

PHPUnit will discover and execute all the tests in your project and provide a summary of the test results.

Symfony's Testing Tools

Symfony provides a set of testing tools and classes to simplify the process of testing your applications. These tools include the Symfony Kernel, the WebTestCase class, and various testing utilities.

Symfony's Kernel allows you to boot your application in a test environment, making it easier to interact with Symfony services and components during testing.

The WebTestCase class extends PHPUnit and provides methods for creating test client instances and making HTTP requests to your application.

```
use Symfony\Bundle\FrameworkBundle\Test\WebTestCase;

class UserControllerTest extends WebTestCase

{

public function testUserRegistration()

{

$client = static::createClient();

$crawler = $client->request('GET', '/register');

$this->assertResponseIsSuccessful();

$this->assertSelectorTextContains('h1', 'User Registration');

}

}
```

Conclusion

Unit testing is a critical part of Symfony development, helping you identify and fix issues early in the development process. PHPUnit is a powerful and widely used tool for writing and running unit tests in Symfony projects. By following best practices and leveraging Symfony's testing tools, you can ensure the reliability and quality of your Symfony applications.

Chapter 7: Templating Engines and Front-end Integration

Section 7.1: Working with Templating Engines

Templating engines play a crucial role in separating the presentation layer from the application logic in web development. Symfony, a popular PHP framework, provides a powerful templating engine called Twig. In this section, we'll explore the basics of working with Twig and how to integrate it into your Symfony project.

Understanding Templating Engines

Templating engines are tools that allow developers to create dynamic and reusable templates for generating HTML, XML, or other markup languages. These templates often include placeholders or variables that get replaced with actual data when rendering the final output.

Twig is a modern and feature-rich templating engine used extensively in Symfony projects. It provides a clean and secure way to define templates with a syntax that is easy to read and write.

Installing and Configuring Twig

In Symfony, Twig is included by default, so you don't need to install it separately. However, you may need to configure it based on your project's needs.

Twig configuration settings are typically defined in the config/packages/twig.yaml file. You can customize settings like template paths, cache settings, and more in this file.

```
# config/packages/twig.yaml

twig:

paths:

'%kernel.project_dir%/templates': templates

debug: '%kernel.debug%'

strict_variables: '%kernel.debug%'
```

In the above example, we specify the template path and set the debug and strict_variables options based on the kernel's debug mode.

Creating Twig Templates

Twig templates are stored in the templates directory of your Symfony project. You can create a new Twig template by adding a .twig extension to your template file, such as my_template.twig.

Here's a simple example of a Twig template:

```
{# templates/welcome.twig #}

<!DOCTYPE html>

<html>

<head>

<title>Welcome</title>

</head>

<body>

<h1>Hello, {{ name }}!</h1>
```

```
</body>

</html>
```

In this template, we use {{ name }} as a placeholder for dynamic content.

Rendering Twig Templates

To render a Twig template in your Symfony controller, you can use the render method. First, make sure you have access to the Twig\Environment service, which Symfony provides by default.

```
use Symfony\Bundle\FrameworkBundle\Controller\AbstractController;

use Symfony\Component\HttpFoundation\Response;

use Twig\Environment;

class WelcomeController extends AbstractController

{

public function welcome(Environment $twig): Response

{

return new Response(

$twig->render('welcome.twig', ['name' => 'John'])

);

}

}
```

In this example, we inject the Twig\Environment service into the controller and use it to render the welcome.twig template, passing the name variable as context data.

Twig Features and Syntax

Twig offers various features and a clean syntax for template creation. You can use conditionals, loops, filters, and more to build complex templates. Twig also provides powerful escaping mechanisms to prevent cross-site scripting (XSS) attacks by default.

```
{# Example of Twig features #}

<ul>

{% for fruit in fruits %}

<li>{{ fruit | upper }}</li>

{% endfor %}

</ul>
```

In this example, we use a for loop to iterate over an array of fruits and apply the upper filter to capitalize each fruit's name before displaying it.

Conclusion

Twig is a versatile templating engine that simplifies the process of creating dynamic and secure templates in Symfony. By understanding its syntax and features, you can build elegant and maintainable templates for your web applications, ensuring a clear separation of concerns between the presentation and logic layers of your project.

Section 7.2: Integrating PHP with HTML5 and CSS3

Integrating PHP with HTML5 and CSS3 is a fundamental aspect of web development. PHP is often used to generate dynamic HTML content while HTML5 and CSS3 provide the structure and styling for web pages. In this section, we'll explore how PHP can be seamlessly integrated with HTML5 and CSS3 to create dynamic and visually appealing web applications.

Embedding PHP in HTML

One of the most common ways to integrate PHP with HTML5 is by embedding PHP code directly within HTML files. PHP code is enclosed within <?php and ?> tags, allowing you to execute PHP logic and generate dynamic content within HTML.

```
<!DOCTYPE html>

<html>

<head>

<title>Dynamic Page</title>

</head>

<body>

<h1>Welcome, <?php echo "John"; ?></h1>

</body>

</html>
```

In this example, PHP is used to insert the name "John" dynamically into the HTML <h1> element.

Separation of Concerns

While embedding PHP within HTML is a quick way to generate dynamic content, it's essential to maintain a clear separation of concerns. This separation ensures that code remains maintainable and follows best practices.

A common practice is to use the Model-View-Controller (MVC) architecture. PHP code handles the application's logic (Model and Controller), while HTML and CSS handle the presentation (View). This separation makes it easier to update and maintain code in the long run.

PHP Templating Engines

To achieve a better separation of concerns and improve code maintainability, you can use PHP templating engines such as Twig (as discussed in the previous section). These templating engines provide a clean and organized way to generate dynamic HTML content within PHP.

```
<!DOCTYPE html>

<html>

<head>

<title>Welcome</title>

</head>

<body>

<h1>Hello, {{ name }}!</h1>

</body>
```

```
</html>
```

In this Twig template, the dynamic content is enclosed in {{ }} placeholders, making it more readable and maintainable.

External CSS Files

CSS3 is used to style web pages, and it's best practice to keep CSS styles in separate external files. This separation allows for better organization and reuse of styles across multiple pages.

```
<!DOCTYPE html>

<html>

<head>

<link rel="stylesheet" type="text/css" href="styles.css">

<title>Styled Page</title>

</head>

<body>

<h1>Welcome, John!</h1>

</body>

</html>
```

In this example, the <link> tag references an external CSS file named styles.css, which contains the styling rules for the page.

Dynamic CSS with PHP

You can also generate dynamic CSS using PHP. For instance, you can create CSS rules based on user preferences or application data.

```
<?php
header("Content-type: text/css");
$primaryColor = "#007bff";
?>
body {
background-color: <?php echo $primaryColor; ?>;
color: white;
}
```

In this example, PHP sets the $primaryColor variable, which is used to dynamically generate the background color of the <body> element in the CSS.

Conclusion

Integrating PHP with HTML5 and CSS3 is a fundamental skill for web developers. By understanding how to embed PHP in HTML, maintain separation of concerns, use PHP templating engines, and generate dynamic CSS, you can create dynamic and visually appealing web applications that provide a seamless user experience.

Section 7.3: JavaScript and PHP: Creating Interactive Web Pages

Combining JavaScript and PHP is a powerful way to create interactive web pages. While PHP handles server-side processing and dynamic content generation, JavaScript enhances the user experience by enabling client-side interactivity. In this section, we'll explore how to integrate JavaScript and PHP to create dynamic and engaging web applications.

Client-Side vs. Server-Side

Before diving into integration, it's essential to understand the distinction between client-side and server-side scripting. PHP operates on the server and generates HTML that is sent to the client's browser. JavaScript, on the other hand, runs in the client's browser and can manipulate the HTML and respond to user actions dynamically.

Asynchronous Requests with AJAX

One common integration point for JavaScript and PHP is Asynchronous JavaScript and XML (AJAX). AJAX allows you to make asynchronous requests to the server without requiring a full page reload. This enables dynamic content updates without interrupting the user's experience.

```
// JavaScript code for making an AJAX request to a PHP script

var xhr = new XMLHttpRequest();

xhr.open('GET', 'server.php', true);

xhr.onreadystatechange = function () {

if (xhr.readyState === 4 && xhr.status === 200) {

var response = xhr.responseText;

// Handle the response here (e.g., update the page content)

document.getElementById('result').innerHTML = response;

}
```

```
};

xhr.send();
```

In this example, JavaScript makes an AJAX request to a PHP script (server.php) and updates the page's content with the response.

Passing Data Between JavaScript and PHP

To pass data between JavaScript and PHP, you can use techniques like AJAX to send data from JavaScript to a PHP script for processing. Conversely, you can generate JavaScript code dynamically using PHP to provide data to your JavaScript functions.

```
// JavaScript code to send data to PHP via AJAX

var data = { username: 'John', email: 'john@example.com' };

var xhr = new XMLHttpRequest();

xhr.open('POST', 'process.php', true);

xhr.setRequestHeader('Content-Type', 'application/json');

xhr.onreadystatechange = function () {

if (xhr.readyState === 4 && xhr.status === 200) {

var response = xhr.responseText;

// Handle the response from PHP

console.log(response);

}

};

xhr.send(JSON.stringify(data));
```

In this example, JavaScript sends JSON data to a PHP script (process.php) via an AJAX POST request.

Server-Side JavaScript Execution with Node.js

While JavaScript is traditionally a client-side language, Node.js allows you to execute JavaScript on the server-side. This means you can use JavaScript for both client and server logic, creating a unified development environment. However, PHP and Node.js have different use cases, and choosing one depends on your project's requirements.

Conclusion

Integrating JavaScript and PHP opens up a world of possibilities for creating dynamic and interactive web applications. Whether you're making AJAX requests, passing data between the two languages, or exploring server-side JavaScript with Node.js, this combination empowers you to build engaging user interfaces and provide seamless user experiences. Understanding when and how to use each language is key to successful integration and web development.

Section 7.4: Using AJAX with PHP

AJAX (Asynchronous JavaScript and XML) is a powerful technology that allows you to make asynchronous requests to the server from your web page without the need for a full page reload. It's widely used to create dynamic and responsive web applications. In this section, we will explore how to use AJAX with PHP to enhance your web applications.

Understanding AJAX

AJAX is a technique that leverages JavaScript to send HTTP requests to the server and retrieve data or perform actions without reloading the entire web page. This enables seamless and interactive user experiences. AJAX can be used with various HTTP methods, such as GET and POST, to fetch or send data to the server.

Creating an AJAX Request

To create an AJAX request in JavaScript, you typically use the XMLHttpRequest object or the newer fetch API. Here's an example using XMLHttpRequest to make a GET request to a PHP script and update the page with the response:

```
var xhr = new XMLHttpRequest();
xhr.open('GET', 'example.php', true);
xhr.onreadystatechange = function () {
if (xhr.readyState === 4 && xhr.status === 200) {
var response = xhr.responseText;
// Update the page with the response data
document.getElementById('result').innerHTML = response;
}
};
xhr.send();
```

In this example, we create an XMLHttpRequest object, specify the request method and URL, and define a callback function to handle the response.

Handling AJAX Requests in PHP

On the server-side, you can handle AJAX requests in a PHP script (example.php in the example above). PHP processes the request and sends back a response, which can be plain text, JSON, or other formats. Here's a basic PHP script that responds to an AJAX request:

```
<?php

// Perform server-side processing

$data = ['message' => 'Hello from PHP!'];

header('Content-Type: application/json');

echo json_encode($data);

?>
```

In this PHP script, we perform some server-side processing and respond with a JSON-encoded message. The header function sets the response's content type to JSON.

Handling POST Requests

AJAX can also be used for sending data to the server using the POST method. Here's an example of making a POST request with JavaScript:

```
var xhr = new XMLHttpRequest();

xhr.open('POST', 'submit.php', true);
```

```
xhr.setRequestHeader('Content-Type', 'application/x-www-form-urlencoded');

xhr.onreadystatechange = function () {

if (xhr.readyState === 4 && xhr.status === 200) {

var response = xhr.responseText;

// Handle the response from PHP

}

};

var data = 'username=johndoe&email=johndoe@example.com';

xhr.send(data);
```

In this example, we set the request method to POST and include data in the request body. On the PHP side, you can access this data using the $_POST superglobal.

Conclusion

AJAX and PHP complement each other to create dynamic and responsive web applications. By making asynchronous requests to PHP scripts, you can fetch and update data without reloading the entire page, providing a more engaging user experience. Understanding how to use AJAX effectively with PHP is a valuable skill for modern web development.

Section 7.5: Responsive Web Design Principles

Responsive web design is a crucial aspect of modern web development. It ensures that websites look and function well on various devices and screen sizes, from large desktop monitors to smartphones and tablets. In this section, we will explore the principles of responsive web design and how to implement them effectively.

Understanding Responsive Design

Responsive design is a web design approach that aims to create flexible layouts and adapt the content to different viewport sizes. It ensures that the user experience remains consistent and user-friendly across a wide range of devices. The key principles of responsive design include fluid grids, flexible images, and media queries.

Fluid Grids

A fluid grid is the foundation of responsive design. Instead of fixed pixel-based layouts, responsive websites use relative units like percentages to define the width of elements. This allows content to adjust proportionally to the screen size. For example, a container set to 50% width will always occupy half of the viewport's width, whether on a desktop or mobile device.

```
.container {
width: 100%;
}
.column {
```

```
width: 50%;

float: left;

}
```

In the above CSS example, the container and columns use percentage-based widths to create a flexible grid.

Flexible Images

Images play a significant role in web design, and they need to adapt to different screen sizes. To make images responsive, use the max-width: 100%; property to ensure they never exceed their container's width. This prevents images from overflowing or distorting the layout on smaller screens.

```
img {

max-width: 100%;

height: auto;

}
```

With this CSS rule, images will scale down proportionally to fit their container.

Media Queries

Media queries are CSS techniques that allow you to apply specific styles based on the user's device characteristics, such as screen width, height, and orientation. They enable you to create different layouts and styles for various screen sizes. Here's an example of a media query targeting screens with a maximum width of 768 pixels:

```
@media screen and (max-width: 768px) {
```

```
/* CSS rules for smaller screens */
}
```

Within a media query block, you can adjust font sizes, margins, padding, and other styling to optimize the design for smaller screens.

Testing and Debugging

Responsive web design requires thorough testing across different devices and screen sizes. Tools like browser developer tools, emulators, and real device testing help identify and fix issues. Ensure that touch events work on mobile devices and that content remains readable and accessible.

Conclusion

Responsive web design is essential in today's multi-device world. By applying fluid grids, flexible images, and media queries, you can create websites that adapt seamlessly to various screens and provide an optimal user experience. Prioritizing responsive design principles ensures your web content looks and functions its best, regardless of the device your audience uses.

Chapter 8: Content Management Systems in PHP

Section 8.1: Introduction to CMS

A Content Management System (CMS) is a software application that allows users to create, manage, and publish digital content, such as websites, blogs, and online stores, without the need for extensive coding or technical expertise. CMS platforms have become increasingly popular due to their ease of use and flexibility. In this section, we will introduce the concept of CMS and explore its significance in web development.

What is a CMS?

At its core, a CMS is designed to simplify the process of content creation and management for individuals and organizations. It provides a user-friendly interface that allows non-technical users to add, edit, and organize content easily. This content can include text, images, videos, and other multimedia elements.

Key Features of CMS

1. **Content Authoring:** CMS platforms offer WYSIWYG (What You See Is What You Get) editors, making it simple for users to create and format content without any HTML or coding knowledge.
2. **Content Organization:** CMS systems enable content to be organized into categories, tags, and hierarchies, making it easy to maintain a structured website.
3. **User Management:** CMS platforms often include user management features, allowing administrators to control

who can access and edit content on the site.

4. **Version Control:** Many CMSs offer version control, allowing users to revert to previous versions of content if needed.
5. **Extensibility:** CMSs can be extended with plugins, themes, and custom code to add additional functionality and customize the appearance of a website.

Popular CMS Platforms

There are numerous CMS platforms available, each with its strengths and weaknesses. Some of the most widely used CMSs in PHP web development include:

- **WordPress:** Known for its simplicity and versatility, WordPress is often used for blogs, business websites, and e-commerce stores. It has a large community and an extensive library of plugins and themes.

- **Joomla:** Joomla is a powerful and flexible CMS suitable for various types of websites, including corporate sites, online magazines, and e-commerce stores. It offers robust user management and content organization features.

- **Drupal:** Drupal is a highly customizable CMS favored for large and complex websites. It provides excellent security features, making it suitable for government, education, and enterprise websites.

- **Magento:** Magento is a dedicated e-commerce CMS known for its scalability and extensive e-commerce features. It is commonly used for building online stores and marketplaces.

The Role of PHP in CMS Development

Many CMS platforms, including WordPress, Joomla, and Drupal, are built using PHP as their primary programming language. PHP's flexibility, performance, and support for a wide range of databases make it a popular choice for developing CMSs. Understanding PHP is essential for customizing and extending CMS functionality.

Conclusion

Content Management Systems have revolutionized the way websites are created and managed. They empower individuals and organizations to build and maintain digital content efficiently. In the following sections, we will delve deeper into specific CMS platforms, including WordPress, Joomla, and Drupal, and explore how to leverage PHP to customize and extend their capabilities to meet specific project requirements.

Section 8.2: Building Websites with WordPress

WordPress is one of the most popular and widely used Content Management Systems (CMS) in the world. It started as a blogging platform but has evolved into a versatile CMS capable of powering various types of websites, from blogs and business sites to e-commerce stores and more. In this section, we'll explore how to build websites using WordPress and its PHP-based architecture.

Installing WordPress

To get started with WordPress, you need to install it on your web server. Here's a basic outline of the installation process:

1. **Download WordPress:** Visit the official WordPress

website and download the latest version of WordPress.

2. **Create a Database:** You'll need a MySQL database for WordPress to store your site's content. Create a new database and user with the necessary privileges.
3. **Configuration File:** Rename the wp-config-sample.php file to wp-config.php and provide the database details you created in the previous step.
4. **Upload Files:** Upload all the WordPress files to your web server using FTP or a file manager provided by your hosting provider.
5. **Run the Installer:** Access your website in a web browser, and WordPress will guide you through the installation process. You'll set up the admin user and other site details during this step.

Once WordPress is installed, you can log in to the admin dashboard, where you can start customizing your website and creating content.

Themes and Templates

WordPress offers a wide range of themes that determine the design and layout of your website. You can choose from free and premium themes or create custom themes using PHP, HTML, CSS, and JavaScript. WordPress uses a template system where PHP files define how different types of content are displayed.

Here's an example of a simple WordPress template file (single.php) that displays a single post:

```
<?php get_header(); ?>

<div id="content">

<?php while (have_posts()) : the_post(); ?>
```

```
<div class="post">
<h2><?php the_title(); ?></h2>
<div class="post-content">
<?php the_content(); ?>
</div>
</div>
<?php endwhile; ?>
</div>
<?php get_sidebar(); ?>
<?php get_footer(); ?>
```

Plugins and Functionality

WordPress's functionality can be extended using plugins. There are thousands of free and premium plugins available to add features like contact forms, SEO optimization, e-commerce, social media integration, and more. You can also develop your custom plugins in PHP to meet specific requirements.

Here's an example of a simple WordPress plugin that adds a custom widget to display recent posts:

```
function custom_recent_posts_widget() {
register_widget('Custom_Recent_Posts_Widget');
}
class Custom_Recent_Posts_Widget extends WP_Widget {
```

```
// Widget constructor and methods here
}
add_action('widgets_init', 'custom_recent_posts_widget');
```

Customization and Development

Customizing WordPress often involves writing PHP code to create custom themes, plugins, or functionality. WordPress provides extensive documentation and a developer-friendly ecosystem, making it accessible for PHP developers to work with.

In conclusion, WordPress, powered by PHP, is a versatile CMS that allows you to build a wide range of websites. Whether you're a beginner or an experienced developer, WordPress offers the flexibility and tools needed to create and customize websites efficiently. Understanding PHP is valuable when you want to extend WordPress's capabilities or develop custom themes and plugins tailored to your project's needs.

Section 8.3: Customizing Joomla for Web Projects

Joomla is another popular Content Management System (CMS) written in PHP, known for its flexibility and extensibility. In this section, we'll explore how to customize Joomla for various web projects, harnessing the power of PHP to tailor your websites or web applications to specific requirements.

Getting Started with Joomla

Before diving into customization, it's essential to get acquainted with Joomla's basics. Here's a brief overview:

1. **Installation:** Begin by installing Joomla on your web server. Download the latest version, create a database, and follow the installation wizard to set up your Joomla site.
2. **User Management:** Joomla provides a user management system, allowing you to define different user roles and access levels for administrators, editors, and regular users.
3. **Content Creation:** You can create and organize content using articles, categories, and tags. Joomla offers a user-friendly content editor for text formatting and media embedding.
4. **Extensions:** Joomla's power lies in its extensions. These include components, modules, and plugins that add functionality to your site. You can find various extensions in the Joomla Extensions Directory (JED).

Template Customization

Joomla uses templates to define the look and layout of your website. Customizing templates is a common practice to give your site a unique appearance. Templates are usually written in PHP, HTML, CSS, and JavaScript.

Here's an example of a simple template override in Joomla. Let's say you want to customize the way article titles are displayed. Create a file named override.php in your template's folder and add the following code:

```
<?php

defined('_JEXEC') or die;

// Check if the article has a title

if (!empty($this->item->title)) :
```

```
?>

<h2><?php echo $this->item->title; ?></h2>

<?php endif; ?>
```

By doing this, you've overridden the default behavior for displaying article titles. Now, Joomla will use your custom code to handle title rendering.

Component Development

If your web project requires specific functionality that is not available through existing extensions, you can develop your Joomla components. Components are more complex extensions that often require PHP programming skills.

Here's a simplified example of a Joomla component that displays a list of products:

```
<?php

defined('_JEXEC') or die;

class com_products

{

public function display()

{

// Fetch products from the database

$products = $this->getProducts();

// Render the product list
```

```
include JPATH_COMPONENT . '/views/products/tmpl/default.php';

}

private function getProducts()

{

// Database query to retrieve product data

// Return an array of product objects

}

}
```

Joomla Extension Development

In addition to components, Joomla supports the creation of modules and plugins, all of which can be written in PHP to extend the functionality of your website. Joomla's development documentation provides detailed guidance on creating these extensions.

Customizing Joomla for web projects involves understanding the Joomla framework, template customization, and potentially developing custom components or extensions. PHP plays a crucial role in this customization process, allowing you to tailor your Joomla site to meet your project's specific requirements.

Section 8.4: Drupal: Advanced Site Building

Drupal is a powerful and highly customizable Content Management System (CMS) written in PHP. In this section, we'll explore advanced site-building techniques in Drupal, leveraging PHP and Drupal's extensive module system to create feature-rich websites.

Drupal Modules and Extensions

One of Drupal's strengths is its modular architecture. Drupal's functionality can be extended through modules, and there are thousands of contributed modules available on Drupal.org. These modules can range from simple utilities to complex, feature-rich applications.

Here's how you can use PHP to work with Drupal modules:

1. **Installing Modules:** You can install modules via the Drupal administration interface or manually by placing them in the sites/all/modules directory. Enabling modules allows you to use their functionality.
2. **Custom Module Development:** If you have specific requirements not met by existing modules, you can create custom modules using PHP. Drupal provides an extensive API that allows you to interact with the system, create custom content types, and define new functionality.

Here's a simple example of a custom Drupal module:

```
/**

* Implements hook_menu() to define a custom page callback.

*/

function mymodule_menu() {

$items = array();

$items['custom-page'] = array(

'title' => 'Custom Page',
```

```
'page callback' => 'drupal_get_form',
'page arguments' => array('mymodule_custom_page_form'),
'access arguments' => array('access content'),
'type' => MENU_NORMAL_ITEM,
);
return $items;
}
/**
* Callback function to display a custom form.
*/
function mymodule_custom_page_form() {
return drupal_get_form('mymodule_custom_form');
}
/**
* Define a simple form.
*/
function mymodule_custom_form($form, &$form_state) {
$form['message'] = array(
```

```
'#markup' => '<p>Hello, this is a custom form in Drupal!</p>',

);

return $form;

}
```

Theming in Drupal

Theming in Drupal allows you to control the presentation layer of your website. Drupal themes are usually a combination of HTML, CSS, JavaScript, and PHP templates. PHP templates are used to dynamically generate HTML content based on Drupal data.

Here's a simple example of a PHP template in a Drupal theme:

```
<?php if ($page['sidebar_first']): ?>

<div id="sidebar-first" class="column sidebar">

<?php print render($page['sidebar_first']); ?>

</div>

<?php endif; ?>
```

In this code, we check if the sidebar_first region is populated and, if so, render its content within a <div> element. This allows for flexible and dynamic theming.

Custom Content Types and Fields

Drupal allows you to create custom content types and fields through its administration interface or programmatically using PHP. This flexibility is particularly useful when building complex websites or web applications with unique content structures.

PHP can be used to define custom content types and fields in code, allowing for version control and automated deployment of content structures. This is often done in a custom module using the hook_node_info() and hook_field_info() functions.

Advanced Site Building Techniques

Drupal offers a wide range of site-building tools and techniques beyond the basics. Some advanced topics you might explore include:

- **Views:** Creating custom views to display content in various ways.
- **Rules:** Defining complex workflows and automation.
- **Entity API:** Customizing and extending entities in Drupal.
- **Caching and Performance Optimization:** Using PHP to optimize Drupal's caching and performance.

In conclusion, Drupal provides a robust platform for advanced site building using PHP. By leveraging Drupal's modular architecture, custom modules, theming, and content structuring, you can create highly customized and feature-rich websites and web applications tailored to your project's requirements.

Section 8.5: E-commerce Solutions with PHP

E-commerce is a booming sector, and PHP offers a plethora of tools and frameworks to build robust online stores and e-commerce platforms. In this section, we'll explore some of the key aspects of building e-commerce solutions using PHP.

Choosing the Right E-commerce Framework

When venturing into e-commerce development with PHP, choosing the right framework is crucial. Several popular PHP e-commerce frameworks are widely used, such as:

1. **WooCommerce:** If you're working with WordPress, WooCommerce is a popular choice. It seamlessly integrates with WordPress and offers a wide range of extensions for additional functionality.
2. **Magento:** Magento is a powerful and highly customizable e-commerce platform built with PHP. It's suitable for both small and large online stores and offers a rich set of features.
3. **OpenCart:** OpenCart is a lightweight and user-friendly PHP e-commerce solution. It's known for its simplicity and ease of use, making it a great choice for smaller businesses.
4. **PrestaShop:** PrestaShop is an open-source e-commerce platform that provides a comprehensive set of features, including multi-language support and a vast library of modules and templates.
5. **Custom Solutions:** For unique or highly specialized e-commerce projects, building a custom solution using PHP and frameworks like Symfony, Laravel, or Yii can be a viable option.

Essential E-commerce Features

Regardless of the framework chosen, there are several essential features that every e-commerce website should have:

1. Product Catalog and Management

Implementing a product catalog with features like product categories, search, filters, and product details pages is fundamental. PHP can be used to create and manage product listings, including product descriptions, images, and pricing.

2. Shopping Cart and Checkout

Building a robust shopping cart system is crucial for e-commerce. PHP can be used to handle shopping cart functionality, including adding and removing items, calculating totals, and managing the checkout process, including payment gateways integration.

3. User Authentication and Profiles

User authentication and registration systems are essential for tracking orders and providing personalized experiences. PHP can manage user account creation, login, and profile management.

4. Payment Integration

Integrating payment gateways securely is a critical part of e-commerce. PHP can be used to handle payment processing, including validating and processing transactions.

5. Order Management

Order processing and management systems are necessary for tracking and fulfilling customer orders. PHP can be employed to create and manage orders, generate invoices, and update order statuses.

6. Security and Data Protection

E-commerce websites deal with sensitive customer information, so security is paramount. PHP can be used to implement security measures such as data encryption, secure payment handling, and protection against common web vulnerabilities.

Leveraging PHP Frameworks

Many PHP frameworks offer pre-built e-commerce modules, extensions, and libraries that can significantly speed up development. For example, Laravel has the Bagisto e-commerce platform built on top of it, while Symfony provides Sylius, a modern e-commerce framework.

These frameworks provide a solid foundation for e-commerce projects, helping developers focus on business logic and customization rather than building everything from scratch.

Mobile Responsiveness and SEO

Ensuring that your e-commerce website is mobile-responsive is crucial, as an increasing number of customers shop on mobile devices. PHP can be used to implement responsive design techniques, optimizing the user experience on various screen sizes.

Additionally, optimizing your e-commerce site for search engines (SEO) is essential for attracting organic traffic. PHP can be employed to generate SEO-friendly URLs, implement meta tags, and create sitemaps.

In conclusion, PHP is a versatile and powerful language for developing e-commerce solutions. Whether you choose an existing e-commerce framework or opt for a custom solution, PHP's flexibility and extensive ecosystem of libraries and tools make it a great choice for building online stores and e-commerce platforms that meet your specific business needs.

Chapter 9: PHP 7 and Cloud Computing

Section 9.1: Understanding Cloud Computing Concepts

Cloud computing has revolutionized the way applications and services are deployed and managed. It offers scalability, flexibility, and cost-efficiency, making it a popular choice for businesses of all sizes. In this section, we will explore the fundamentals of cloud computing and how PHP 7 can be leveraged in cloud-based solutions.

What Is Cloud Computing?

At its core, cloud computing is the delivery of various computing services over the internet. These services can include servers, storage, databases, networking, software, analytics, and more. Cloud providers like Amazon Web Services (AWS), Microsoft Azure, Google Cloud Platform (GCP), and others offer these services on a pay-as-you-go basis.

Key Concepts in Cloud Computing

1. **On-Demand Self-Service:** Cloud resources can be provisioned and managed by users as needed. This eliminates the need for upfront investments in hardware and infrastructure.
2. **Scalability:** Cloud services are highly scalable, allowing businesses to scale up or down based on demand. This ensures optimal resource utilization and cost-efficiency.
3. **Resource Pooling:** Cloud providers use multi-tenant

models where resources are shared among multiple users. This pooling of resources results in cost savings and efficient resource utilization.

4. **Elasticity:** Elasticity is the ability to automatically adjust resource allocation based on workload. This ensures that applications can handle varying levels of traffic without manual intervention.
5. **Measured Service:** Cloud resources are metered, and users are billed based on their actual usage. This pay-as-you-go model is cost-effective and transparent.

Cloud Service Models

Cloud computing offers several service models, including:

1. **Infrastructure as a Service (IaaS):** IaaS provides virtualized computing resources over the internet. Users can rent virtual machines, storage, and networking resources. PHP applications running on IaaS can have full control over the underlying infrastructure.
2. **Platform as a Service (PaaS):** PaaS provides a platform that allows developers to build, deploy, and manage applications without worrying about the underlying infrastructure. PHP developers can focus solely on coding and application logic.
3. **Software as a Service (SaaS):** SaaS delivers software applications over the internet on a subscription basis. Users access the software through a web browser. PHP may be used to develop SaaS applications hosted in the cloud.

Benefits of Cloud Computing

Cloud computing offers numerous benefits for PHP developers and businesses:

- **Cost-Efficiency:** Cloud services eliminate the need for upfront hardware investments and reduce operational costs.

- **Scalability:** Businesses can easily scale their PHP applications to accommodate changing workloads.

- **Flexibility:** Cloud platforms offer a wide range of services and tools, allowing PHP developers to choose the best tools for their projects.

- **Reliability:** Cloud providers offer high availability and disaster recovery options, ensuring that PHP applications remain accessible even in case of failures.

- **Global Reach:** Cloud providers have data centers worldwide, allowing businesses to deploy PHP applications in multiple regions for improved performance and redundancy.

Common Cloud Deployment Scenarios with PHP

PHP applications can be deployed in various cloud deployment models, including:

- **Public Cloud:** PHP applications run on cloud infrastructure provided by third-party vendors. This is a cost-effective option for many businesses.

- **Private Cloud:** Some businesses choose to set up their own private cloud infrastructure to host PHP applications. This offers more control but requires significant investment.

- **Hybrid Cloud:** A combination of public and private clouds is used to host PHP applications. This allows businesses to leverage both the cost-efficiency of public clouds and the control of private clouds.

In conclusion, cloud computing is a transformative technology that has reshaped the IT landscape. PHP 7, with its performance improvements and versatility, is well-suited for developing cloud-based applications and services. Understanding cloud computing concepts and the various deployment models is essential for PHP developers looking to harness the power of the cloud.

Section 9.2: Deploying PHP Applications on the Cloud

Once you have a grasp of cloud computing concepts, the next step is to understand how to deploy PHP applications on cloud platforms. This section will guide you through the process and best practices for deploying your PHP applications in the cloud.

Choose the Right Cloud Provider

Before deploying your PHP application, you need to choose a cloud provider that aligns with your project's requirements. Some popular cloud providers for PHP applications are AWS, Azure, Google Cloud, and DigitalOcean. Each has its own set of services and pricing models, so consider factors such as scalability, geographic regions, and budget when making your choice.

Preparing Your PHP Application

Before deploying your PHP application to the cloud, make sure it's ready for the cloud environment. Here are some key steps:

1. **Code Optimization:** Optimize your PHP code for performance. This includes minimizing database queries, enabling opcode caching, and using appropriate design patterns.
2. **Dependency Management:** Use tools like Composer to manage dependencies efficiently. Ensure your composer.json file is up to date.
3. **Environment Configuration:** Implement environment-specific configurations using environment variables. This allows your application to adapt to different cloud environments.
4. **Security Measures:** Implement security best practices, including input validation, user authentication, and data encryption. Cloud environments are secure, but your application should also be secure by design.

Choose a Deployment Model

Select the deployment model that suits your application's needs:

1. **Single Instance Deployment:** Deploy your PHP application on a single virtual machine (VM) instance. This is suitable for small projects with low traffic.
2. **Load-Balanced Deployment:** Use load balancers to distribute traffic across multiple VM instances. This ensures high availability and scalability.
3. **Serverless Deployment:** Consider serverless computing platforms like AWS Lambda or Google Cloud Functions for event-driven applications. You don't need to manage

infrastructure in this model.

Containerization and Orchestration

Containerization with technologies like Docker and container orchestration with Kubernetes are valuable for deploying and managing PHP applications at scale. Containers encapsulate your application and its dependencies, making it easier to move between different cloud environments.

Database Considerations

If your PHP application relies on a database, you should consider database services provided by cloud providers. Services like Amazon RDS, Azure Database for MySQL, and Google Cloud SQL offer managed database solutions that can simplify database administration tasks.

Continuous Integration and Continuous Deployment (CI/CD)

Implement CI/CD pipelines to automate the deployment process. Tools like Jenkins, Travis CI, or GitLab CI/CD can help you build, test, and deploy your PHP application to the cloud automatically whenever changes are pushed to your repository.

Monitoring and Scaling

Cloud providers offer monitoring and scaling solutions to ensure your PHP application's performance and availability. Use cloud-native monitoring tools or integrate third-party monitoring solutions to keep an eye on your application's health.

Backup and Disaster Recovery

Plan for backup and disaster recovery. Most cloud providers offer backup and snapshot capabilities. Regularly back up your data and implement disaster recovery strategies to minimize downtime.

Cost Optimization

Keep an eye on costs. Monitor your cloud resource usage and consider reserved instances or spot instances for cost savings. Make use of cloud provider cost management tools to optimize your spending.

Conclusion

Deploying PHP applications in the cloud offers numerous advantages in terms of scalability, reliability, and flexibility. By choosing the right cloud provider, preparing your application, and following best practices for deployment and management, you can leverage the power of cloud computing to run your PHP applications efficiently and cost-effectively.

Section 9.3: Working with AWS and PHP

Amazon Web Services (AWS) is one of the leading cloud providers, offering a wide range of services for deploying and managing PHP applications. In this section, we'll explore how to work with AWS and PHP to leverage its cloud services effectively.

AWS Services for PHP Applications

AWS provides various services that are well-suited for hosting and running PHP applications:

1. **Amazon EC2:** Amazon Elastic Compute Cloud (EC2)

allows you to deploy virtual servers (instances) where you can run your PHP applications. You can choose the instance type that fits your application's requirements in terms of CPU, memory, and storage.

2. **AWS Elastic Beanstalk:** Elastic Beanstalk is a Platform as a Service (PaaS) offering that simplifies deploying, managing, and scaling PHP applications. It abstracts the infrastructure management, allowing you to focus on your code.
3. **Amazon RDS:** Amazon Relational Database Service (RDS) provides managed database services for MySQL, PostgreSQL, and other databases. It's an excellent choice for storing your application's data securely.
4. **Amazon S3:** Simple Storage Service (S3) is AWS's object storage service. You can use it to store static assets, backups, and user uploads. It integrates seamlessly with PHP for file storage.
5. **Amazon CloudFront:** CloudFront is a Content Delivery Network (CDN) service that helps distribute your PHP application's content globally for faster delivery to end users.

Setting Up AWS Credentials

To interact with AWS services from your PHP application, you'll need AWS credentials. These credentials consist of an Access Key ID and a Secret Access Key. You can obtain these by creating an IAM (Identity and Access Management) user in your AWS account and assigning the necessary permissions.

Once you have the credentials, you can configure them in your PHP application using the AWS SDK for PHP or other AWS SDKs.

Here's an example of how to set up AWS credentials using the AWS SDK for PHP:

```
require 'vendor/autoload.php'; // Include the AWS SDK for PHP

use Aws\S3\S3Client;

// Specify your AWS credentials

$credentials = [

'key' => 'YOUR_ACCESS_KEY',

'secret' => 'YOUR_SECRET_KEY',

'region' => 'us-east-1', // Replace with your desired AWS region

];

// Create an S3 client with the credentials

$s3 = new S3Client($credentials);
```

Deploying a PHP Application on AWS EC2

To deploy a PHP application on an EC2 instance, follow these steps:

1. **Launch an EC2 instance:** Choose an EC2 instance type that suits your application's requirements. Install PHP, web server software (e.g., Apache or Nginx), and any necessary PHP extensions.
2. **Upload your PHP code:** Use secure methods to transfer your PHP application code to the EC2 instance. You can use SCP, SFTP, or AWS Systems Manager Session Manager for remote access.
3. **Configure security groups:** Ensure that your EC2 instance's security groups allow HTTP or HTTPS traffic

to reach your web server.

4. **Set up a domain:** If you want to use a custom domain, configure DNS settings to point to your EC2 instance's public IP address or associate an Elastic IP address with the instance.
5. **Secure your application:** Implement security best practices, including firewalls, regular updates, and monitoring, to protect your PHP application.

Using AWS Elastic Beanstalk

AWS Elastic Beanstalk simplifies the deployment of PHP applications. You can deploy PHP applications directly from your code repository (e.g., Git) or by uploading a ZIP file. Elastic Beanstalk handles the provisioning of resources, load balancing, and auto-scaling for you.

Here's a basic overview of deploying a PHP application using Elastic Beanstalk:

1. **Create an Elastic Beanstalk environment:** Use the AWS Management Console or the AWS CLI to create an Elastic Beanstalk environment and choose PHP as the platform.
2. **Upload your PHP code:** Deploy your PHP application code to the Elastic Beanstalk environment.
3. **Configure environment variables:** Use Elastic Beanstalk's environment variables to manage configuration settings like database connection strings or API keys.
4. **Scale your application:** Elastic Beanstalk can automatically scale your application based on traffic. You can configure auto-scaling policies as needed.
5. **Monitor and troubleshoot:** Use AWS CloudWatch and Elastic Beanstalk logs to monitor and troubleshoot your

PHP application.

AWS provides detailed documentation and resources for each service to help you get started with deploying and managing PHP applications effectively. By leveraging AWS services, you can build robust and scalable PHP applications in the cloud.

Section 9.4: PHP and Azure: A Comprehensive Guide

Microsoft Azure is another prominent cloud computing platform that offers a range of services for hosting and managing PHP applications. In this section, we'll explore how to work with Azure and PHP, covering key concepts and practical steps.

Azure Services for PHP Applications

Azure provides several services suitable for hosting and running PHP applications:

1. **Azure App Service:** Azure's fully managed platform for building, deploying, and scaling web apps. You can easily deploy PHP applications to Azure App Service, which supports PHP out of the box.
2. **Azure Virtual Machines (VMs):** Similar to AWS EC2, Azure VMs allow you to run PHP applications on virtualized servers. You have flexibility in choosing VM sizes, OS, and PHP configurations.
3. **Azure Functions:** Azure Functions is a serverless compute service that lets you run event-triggered code without managing infrastructure. You can build serverless PHP applications using Azure Functions.
4. **Azure Database for MySQL:** Azure offers a managed

MySQL database service, which is an excellent choice for storing data used by PHP applications.

5. **Azure Blob Storage:** Use Azure Blob Storage to store and serve static assets, files, and media used in your PHP applications.

Setting Up Azure Credentials

To interact with Azure services from your PHP application, you'll need Azure credentials, specifically the Azure subscription ID, client ID, client secret, and tenant ID. Here's an example of how to configure Azure credentials for PHP using the Azure SDK:

```
require_once 'vendor/autoload.php'; // Include the Azure SDK for PHP

use MicrosoftAzure\Storage\Common\ServicesBuilder;

// Specify your Azure credentials

$connectionString =
"DefaultEndpointsProtocol=https;AccountName=YOUR_ACCOUNT_

// Create a Blob service client with the credentials

$blobClient =
ServicesBuilder::getInstance()->createBlobService($connectionString);
```

Deploying a PHP Application on Azure App Service

Azure App Service is a popular choice for deploying PHP applications due to its simplicity and scalability. Here are the steps to deploy a PHP application on Azure App Service:

1. **Create an Azure App Service:** Use the Azure Portal to create a new App Service. Choose the PHP runtime and

configure the settings, including the deployment source (e.g., GitHub, Azure DevOps, or local Git).

2. **Deploy your PHP code:** You can deploy your PHP application by pushing your code to the chosen deployment source. Azure will automatically build and deploy your application.
3. **Configure environment settings:** Use Azure App Service's environment variables to manage configuration settings, such as database connection strings and API keys.
4. **Scale your application:** Azure App Service allows you to scale your application horizontally by adding more instances as needed. You can also configure auto-scaling based on metrics like CPU usage.
5. **Monitor and troubleshoot:** Azure provides monitoring and diagnostics tools to help you monitor the performance and troubleshoot issues in your PHP application.

Using Azure Virtual Machines

If you require more control over the server environment for your PHP application, you can deploy it on Azure Virtual Machines (VMs). Here's a high-level overview:

1. **Create an Azure VM:** Use the Azure Portal or Azure CLI to create a virtual machine. You'll need to choose the appropriate VM size, operating system, and PHP configurations.
2. **Deploy your PHP code:** Transfer your PHP application code to the VM using methods like SCP, SFTP, or Azure Blob Storage.
3. **Configure security:** Implement security measures, including firewalls, network security groups, and regular updates, to secure your PHP application on the VM.

4. **Set up a domain:** Configure DNS settings to point your domain to the VM's public IP address or use Azure's DNS services.
5. **Monitor and manage:** Azure provides monitoring and management tools to keep your VM-based PHP application running smoothly.

By leveraging Azure's services and infrastructure, you can deploy, scale, and manage PHP applications effectively, catering to various use cases and requirements. Azure's flexibility makes it a valuable choice for hosting PHP applications in the cloud.

Section 9.5: PHP and Azure: A Comprehensive Guide

Microsoft Azure is another prominent cloud computing platform that offers a range of services for hosting and managing PHP applications. In this section, we'll explore how to work with Azure and PHP, covering key concepts and practical steps.

Azure Services for PHP Applications

Azure provides several services suitable for hosting and running PHP applications:

1. **Azure App Service:** Azure's fully managed platform for building, deploying, and scaling web apps. You can easily deploy PHP applications to Azure App Service, which supports PHP out of the box.
2. **Azure Virtual Machines (VMs):** Similar to AWS EC2, Azure VMs allow you to run PHP applications on virtualized servers. You have flexibility in choosing VM sizes, OS, and PHP configurations.

3. **Azure Functions:** Azure Functions is a serverless compute service that lets you run event-triggered code without managing infrastructure. You can build serverless PHP applications using Azure Functions.
4. **Azure Database for MySQL:** Azure offers a managed MySQL database service, which is an excellent choice for storing data used by PHP applications.
5. **Azure Blob Storage:** Use Azure Blob Storage to store and serve static assets, files, and media used in your PHP applications.

Setting Up Azure Credentials

To interact with Azure services from your PHP application, you'll need Azure credentials, specifically the Azure subscription ID, client ID, client secret, and tenant ID. Here's an example of how to configure Azure credentials for PHP using the Azure SDK:

```
require_once 'vendor/autoload.php'; // Include the Azure SDK for PHP

use MicrosoftAzure\Storage\Common\ServicesBuilder;

// Specify your Azure credentials

$connectionString = "DefaultEndpointsProtocol=https;AccountName=YOUR_ACCOUNT_

// Create a Blob service client with the credentials

$blobClient = ServicesBuilder::getInstance()->createBlobService($connectionString);
```

Deploying a PHP Application on Azure App Service

Azure App Service is a popular choice for deploying PHP applications due to its simplicity and scalability. Here are the steps to deploy a PHP application on Azure App Service:

1. **Create an Azure App Service:** Use the Azure Portal to create a new App Service. Choose the PHP runtime and configure the settings, including the deployment source (e.g., GitHub, Azure DevOps, or local Git).
2. **Deploy your PHP code:** You can deploy your PHP application by pushing your code to the chosen deployment source. Azure will automatically build and deploy your application.
3. **Configure environment settings:** Use Azure App Service's environment variables to manage configuration settings, such as database connection strings and API keys.
4. **Scale your application:** Azure App Service allows you to scale your application horizontally by adding more instances as needed. You can also configure auto-scaling based on metrics like CPU usage.
5. **Monitor and troubleshoot:** Azure provides monitoring and diagnostics tools to help you monitor the performance and troubleshoot issues in your PHP application.

Using Azure Virtual Machines

If you require more control over the server environment for your PHP application, you can deploy it on Azure Virtual Machines (VMs). Here's a high-level overview:

1. **Create an Azure VM:** Use the Azure Portal or Azure CLI to create a virtual machine. You'll need to choose the appropriate VM size, operating system, and PHP

configurations.

2. **Deploy your PHP code:** Transfer your PHP application code to the VM using methods like SCP, SFTP, or Azure Blob Storage.
3. **Configure security:** Implement security measures, including firewalls, network security groups, and regular updates, to secure your PHP application on the VM.
4. **Set up a domain:** Configure DNS settings to point your domain to the VM's public IP address or use Azure's DNS services.
5. **Monitor and manage:** Azure provides monitoring and management tools to keep your VM-based PHP application running smoothly.

By leveraging Azure's services and infrastructure, you can deploy, scale, and manage PHP applications effectively, catering to various use cases and requirements. Azure's flexibility makes it a valuable choice for hosting PHP applications in the cloud.

Chapter 10: PHP 7 and IoT

Section 10.1: Introduction to IoT with PHP

The Internet of Things (IoT) is a revolutionary concept that has gained tremendous momentum in recent years. It refers to the interconnectedness of everyday devices and objects to the internet, allowing them to collect, exchange, and process data. In this section, we'll explore how PHP can be used in the context of IoT and delve into the fundamentals of IoT with PHP.

Understanding IoT and Its Components

IoT involves a multitude of components working together to enable smart and automated systems. Some of the key components of IoT include:

1. **Devices and Sensors:** IoT devices are embedded with sensors that collect data from the physical world. These devices can range from simple temperature sensors to complex industrial machinery.
2. **Connectivity:** IoT devices need a way to transmit data to a central server or cloud platform. Common communication protocols in IoT include Wi-Fi, Bluetooth, cellular networks, and LoRaWAN.
3. **Data Processing:** Data collected from IoT devices is sent to a cloud platform or edge server for processing. This data may be structured or unstructured and can include sensor readings, images, or videos.
4. **Cloud Platforms:** Cloud platforms like AWS IoT, Azure IoT, and Google Cloud IoT provide the infrastructure to manage IoT devices, store data, and run analytics. These

platforms offer various services for device management, data ingestion, and real-time processing.

5. **Applications:** IoT applications are responsible for receiving and interpreting data from devices. These applications can trigger actions based on data analysis, such as sending alerts or adjusting device settings.

PHP's Role in IoT

PHP, as a versatile and widely-used scripting language, can play a significant role in IoT applications:

1. **Web Interfaces:** PHP can be used to develop web-based dashboards and user interfaces for IoT applications. These interfaces allow users to monitor and control IoT devices remotely.
2. **Data Processing:** PHP scripts can be integrated into the data processing pipeline of IoT applications. They can transform and analyze data as it flows from devices to storage or other services.
3. **Device Management:** PHP can be employed to build applications for managing IoT devices. This includes tasks like device registration, configuration, and firmware updates.
4. **Integration with IoT Platforms:** PHP applications can interact with cloud-based IoT platforms through APIs and SDKs. This enables seamless communication between IoT devices and the cloud.

Building IoT Applications with PHP

To illustrate the concept of IoT with PHP, let's consider a simple example:

Suppose you have a temperature and humidity sensor installed in your home. The sensor periodically collects temperature and humidity data and sends it to a cloud platform. A PHP application hosted on the cloud platform processes the data and provides a web-based dashboard for users to view the current conditions.

Here's a simplified PHP script that simulates receiving and displaying sensor data:

```
<?php

// Simulated sensor data (replace with real data)

$temperature = 25.5;

$humidity = 60.2;

// Display data on a web page

echo "Current Temperature: $temperature °C<br>";

echo "Current Humidity: $humidity%<br>";

?>
```

In a real-world scenario, you would replace the simulated data with data received from actual IoT devices.

This example illustrates how PHP can be used to develop the web-based portion of an IoT application, but PHP's role in IoT extends beyond this. PHP can also handle data processing, device management, and integration with IoT platforms, making it a versatile choice for building IoT solutions.

Section 10.2: PHP in IoT Ecosystems

In Section 10.1, we introduced the concept of IoT with PHP and explored its role in developing IoT applications. Now, let's delve deeper into PHP's role within IoT ecosystems and how it interacts with various components and technologies.

IoT Ecosystem Components

An IoT ecosystem consists of multiple layers and components that work together to enable the seamless operation of IoT devices and applications. PHP can play a role in several of these components:

1. **Device Layer:** This layer comprises IoT devices equipped with sensors and actuators. PHP may not run directly on these devices due to resource constraints, but it can communicate with them through APIs or protocols like MQTT.
2. **Connectivity Layer:** IoT devices need to communicate with each other and with cloud services. PHP can facilitate communication by acting as an intermediary, receiving data from devices and relaying it to cloud platforms or other devices.
3. **Edge Computing:** In edge computing scenarios, PHP scripts can run on edge devices such as gateways or edge servers. These scripts can preprocess data, filter it, or perform local analytics before sending it to the cloud. This reduces latency and conserves bandwidth.
4. **Cloud Platform:** Cloud platforms like AWS IoT, Azure IoT, or Google Cloud IoT provide robust infrastructure for managing IoT devices, data storage, and analytics. PHP can interact with these platforms through their APIs or SDKs to retrieve and process data.

5. **Applications:** PHP applications can serve as the user interface for IoT systems. They allow users to monitor device status, control devices, and receive alerts. PHP can also handle data visualization and reporting.

Communication Protocols

Effective communication is vital in IoT ecosystems, and PHP can work with various communication protocols commonly used in IoT:

1. **MQTT:** Message Queuing Telemetry Transport (MQTT) is a lightweight, publish-subscribe messaging protocol ideal for IoT. PHP has libraries like Mosquitto that enable it to both publish and subscribe to MQTT topics, making it suitable for real-time data exchange.
2. **HTTP/HTTPS:** PHP can make HTTP requests to communicate with IoT devices, cloud platforms, or web services. IoT devices often expose RESTful APIs that PHP applications can interact with.
3. **CoAP:** Constrained Application Protocol (CoAP) is a protocol designed for IoT devices with limited resources. PHP can use CoAP libraries to communicate with CoAP-enabled devices.

Security Considerations

Security is a paramount concern in IoT ecosystems, and PHP applications should adhere to best practices to ensure the integrity and confidentiality of data:

1. **Authentication and Authorization:** PHP applications should implement robust authentication and authorization mechanisms to ensure that only authorized users can access IoT devices and data.

2. **Data Encryption:** Data transmitted between PHP applications and IoT devices should be encrypted to prevent eavesdropping and data tampering. HTTPS and MQTT over TLS (MQTTs) are commonly used encryption methods.
3. **Device Security:** IoT devices should be securely provisioned, and default credentials should be changed. PHP applications can play a role in managing device security through device management features.
4. **Access Control:** PHP applications should enforce strict access control policies to prevent unauthorized access to sensitive IoT data or device control functions.
5. **Firmware Updates:** Ensuring that IoT devices have up-to-date firmware with security patches is crucial. PHP can assist in managing and distributing firmware updates.

Scalability and Performance

IoT ecosystems often involve a large number of devices and substantial data throughput. PHP applications must be designed for scalability and performance to handle these demands. Techniques like load balancing, caching, and asynchronous processing can enhance the performance of PHP-based IoT applications.

Conclusion

In this section, we've explored PHP's role within IoT ecosystems and its interaction with various components and technologies. PHP's versatility makes it a valuable tool for building and managing IoT applications, from device communication to data processing and user interfaces. However, developers should always prioritize security, scalability, and performance when integrating PHP into IoT projects to ensure the success of their IoT initiatives.

Section 10.3: Building IoT Applications with PHP

In Section 10.2, we explored PHP's role in IoT ecosystems and how it can communicate with IoT devices and interact with various components. Now, let's delve into the practical aspects of building IoT applications with PHP. We'll discuss key considerations, development steps, and sample use cases.

Key Considerations for IoT Application Development with PHP

Before diving into IoT application development with PHP, it's crucial to consider the following aspects:

1. **IoT Device Compatibility:** Ensure that your IoT devices support communication with PHP or have compatible APIs or protocols.
2. **Data Formats:** Decide on the data formats that your IoT devices will use to transmit data. Common formats include JSON and XML, which can be easily processed with PHP.
3. **Security:** Implement robust security measures to protect IoT devices, data transmission, and storage. Use encryption, authentication, and access control.
4. **Data Storage:** Plan how and where you will store IoT data. You can use databases, cloud storage, or distributed file systems.
5. **Scalability:** Design your PHP application to scale horizontally to accommodate a growing number of IoT devices.

Steps to Build an IoT Application with PHP

Here are the steps to build an IoT application using PHP:

1. Define Use Cases and Requirements

Identify the specific use cases your IoT application will address and gather requirements. Determine what data you need to collect from IoT devices and what actions your application should perform.

2. Choose the Right PHP Framework or Library

Select a PHP framework or library that suits your IoT project's requirements. Popular choices include Laravel, Symfony, and Lumen. These frameworks provide tools for building robust web applications and RESTful APIs, which are essential for IoT communication.

3. Set Up a Development Environment

Configure your development environment with the necessary tools and libraries. You might need PHP, a web server (e.g., Apache or Nginx), a database, and any additional libraries for IoT communication.

4. Device Integration

Implement the code to integrate your IoT devices with the PHP application. Depending on your devices, this may involve using HTTP requests, MQTT, or other communication protocols. Ensure that data is transmitted securely.

5. Data Processing

Receive and process data from IoT devices using PHP scripts. You can parse incoming data, perform validations, and store it in your chosen data storage solution. Additionally, implement data transformation or aggregation as needed.

6. User Interface

If your IoT application requires a user interface, build it using PHP and web development technologies like HTML, CSS, and JavaScript. This interface can be used for device monitoring, control, and data visualization.

7. Security Implementation

Implement robust security measures, including authentication and authorization for users and devices. Encrypt data transmissions and enforce access control to prevent unauthorized access.

8. Testing and Quality Assurance

Thoroughly test your IoT application to ensure that it functions as intended. Perform unit testing, integration testing, and security testing to identify and resolve issues.

9. Deployment

Prepare your IoT application for deployment on a production server or cloud platform. Configure the necessary environment variables and settings to run your application securely.

10. Monitoring and Maintenance

Set up monitoring tools to track the health and performance of your IoT application. Monitor device connectivity, data processing, and server resources. Regularly update and maintain your application to address any issues and incorporate new features.

Sample Use Cases for IoT Applications with PHP

1. **Home Automation:** Build an IoT application that allows users to control smart home devices like lights, thermostats, and security cameras through a web interface.
2. **Environmental Monitoring:** Create an IoT application that collects data from environmental sensors (e.g., temperature, humidity, air quality) and provides real-time monitoring and historical data analysis.
3. **Industrial Automation:** Develop an IoT application for industrial settings that monitors machinery, detects faults, and schedules maintenance based on sensor data.
4. **Healthcare:** Build an IoT healthcare application that collects and analyzes patient data from wearable devices and medical sensors, providing healthcare professionals with insights and alerts.
5. **Agriculture:** Create an IoT application for precision agriculture, allowing farmers to monitor soil conditions, crop health, and irrigation systems remotely.

Building IoT applications with PHP requires a well-thought-out approach, careful planning, and attention to security and scalability. By following these steps and considering your project's specific requirements, you can develop effective and reliable IoT solutions using PHP.

Section 10.4: PHP and MQTT Protocol

In this section, we will explore the use of PHP in conjunction with the MQTT (Message Queuing Telemetry Transport) protocol for building IoT applications. MQTT is a lightweight, publish-subscribe messaging protocol commonly used in IoT scenarios due to its efficiency and low overhead. MQTT enables devices to communicate and exchange data in a flexible and scalable manner.

Understanding MQTT

MQTT operates on the publish-subscribe model, where devices communicate via a central message broker. The key components of MQTT are:

- **Broker:** The MQTT broker is responsible for receiving messages from publishers and forwarding them to subscribers. It acts as a message hub, facilitating communication between devices.

- **Publisher:** Publishers are IoT devices or applications that send messages to specific topics on the broker. A topic is a hierarchical string that defines the message's destination.

- **Subscriber:** Subscribers are devices or applications that subscribe to specific topics on the broker. They receive messages published to the topics they are subscribed to.

Using PHP with MQTT

To integrate PHP with MQTT, you can use the Eclipse Paho MQTT client library, which provides PHP support for MQTT communication. You can install the Paho MQTT library using Composer, a dependency manager for PHP:

```
composer require eclipse/paho.mqtt.php
```

Once installed, you can use the library to create MQTT clients in PHP and interact with MQTT brokers. Here's a basic example of how to use the Paho MQTT library to publish and subscribe to MQTT topics in PHP:

```
<?php

require 'vendor/autoload.php';

use Eclipse\MQTT\Client;

use Eclipse\MQTT\Message;

use Eclipse\MQTT\MessageBuilder;

// Create an MQTT client

$client = new Client('mqtt://broker.example.com');

// Connect to the MQTT broker

$client->connect();

// Publish a message to a topic

$message = MessageBuilder::newMessage()

->topic('sensor/temperature')

->payload('22.5°C')

->build();

$client->publish($message);

// Subscribe to a topic and receive messages

$client->subscribe('sensor/temperature');
```

```
$client->loop(function (Message $message) {
echo "Received message on topic: {$message->getTopic()}\n";
echo "Payload: {$message->getPayload()}\n";
});
// Disconnect from the MQTT broker
$client->disconnect();
```

This code establishes an MQTT connection, publishes a message to the "sensor/temperature" topic, subscribes to the same topic, and processes incoming messages.

MQTT in IoT Applications

MQTT is widely used in various IoT applications, including:

1. **Home Automation:** Control and monitor smart devices in homes, such as lights, thermostats, and security cameras.
2. **Industrial IoT (IIoT):** Collect data from sensors and machinery on the factory floor for process optimization and predictive maintenance.
3. **Environmental Monitoring:** Gather data from environmental sensors to monitor air quality, weather conditions, and pollution levels.
4. **Smart Agriculture:** Monitor soil moisture, crop health, and weather conditions in agriculture for efficient resource management.
5. **Healthcare:** Transmit patient data from wearable devices and medical sensors to healthcare systems for remote monitoring and diagnosis.
6. **Asset Tracking:** Track the location and status of assets,

vehicles, and shipments in logistics and supply chain management.

MQTT's lightweight nature and support for reliable message delivery make it a suitable choice for IoT applications where network bandwidth and device resources are limited.

By leveraging the MQTT protocol and integrating it with PHP using libraries like Eclipse Paho MQTT, you can build scalable and efficient IoT applications that facilitate seamless communication between devices and servers. This enables real-time data exchange, remote control, and intelligent decision-making in various IoT scenarios.

Section 10.5: Case Studies: PHP in IoT Solutions

In this section, we will delve into real-world case studies that highlight the successful integration of PHP in Internet of Things (IoT) solutions. These case studies demonstrate how PHP can be a valuable tool in building IoT applications across various domains.

Case Study 1: Smart Home Automation

Objective: Create a smart home automation system that allows homeowners to remotely control lighting, thermostats, and security cameras using a mobile app.

Solution: PHP was used to develop the backend server that communicates with IoT devices and the mobile app. The server manages user authentication, device control, and data storage. MQTT was employed as the communication protocol between the server and IoT devices. PHP's ability to handle HTTP requests and interact with MQTT brokers made it an ideal choice for this project.

The mobile app communicated with the PHP server via RESTful APIs.

Outcome: The smart home automation system provided homeowners with convenient remote control of their devices. PHP's scalability allowed for the addition of new devices and features over time, making it a flexible solution.

Case Study 2: Industrial IoT (IIoT) Monitoring

Objective: Monitor and analyze data from sensors and machines on a factory floor to optimize production processes and reduce downtime.

Solution: PHP was used to develop a web-based dashboard that visualized real-time data from sensors and machines. MQTT was employed for data transmission between IoT devices and the PHP server. The server processed and stored the data in a database, allowing for historical analysis. PHP's web development capabilities and data processing capabilities were instrumental in building the dashboard.

Outcome: The IIoT monitoring system helped the factory achieve significant cost savings by identifying inefficiencies and predicting maintenance needs. The PHP-based dashboard provided actionable insights to operators and management.

Case Study 3: Environmental Monitoring

Objective: Create an environmental monitoring system that collects data from various sensors and weather stations to track air quality, weather conditions, and pollution levels in a city.

Solution: PHP was used to develop a centralized data collection and analysis platform. MQTT facilitated communication between sensors and the PHP server. The server processed incoming data, performed real-time analysis, and generated reports and alerts. PHP's support for web development enabled the creation of a public dashboard where citizens could access real-time environmental data.

Outcome: The environmental monitoring system improved air quality management and helped citizens make informed decisions. PHP's versatility in handling data processing and web presentation played a crucial role in delivering valuable information to the public.

Case Study 4: Healthcare IoT

Objective: Enable remote monitoring of patients' vital signs using wearable IoT devices and provide healthcare professionals with real-time patient data.

Solution: PHP was used to develop a secure and HIPAA-compliant backend server that received data from wearable IoT devices via MQTT. The server processed the data and made it accessible to healthcare professionals through a web-based interface. PHP's capabilities in handling secure data transmission and web development ensured patient data privacy and accessibility.

Outcome: The healthcare IoT solution improved patient care by allowing healthcare professionals to monitor patients remotely. PHP's role in data processing and secure communication was critical in meeting regulatory requirements.

Case Study 5: Agriculture IoT

Objective: Monitor soil moisture, crop health, and weather conditions in agricultural fields to optimize irrigation and resource usage.

Solution: PHP was employed to develop a web-based platform that integrated data from various IoT sensors and weather stations. MQTT facilitated data transmission to the PHP server, which processed the data, generated recommendations, and provided real-time monitoring. PHP's web development capabilities enabled farmers to access the platform from any device.

Outcome: The agriculture IoT solution led to improved crop yields and resource efficiency. PHP's role in data analysis and web accessibility empowered farmers to make data-driven decisions.

These case studies illustrate the versatility and effectiveness of PHP in IoT solutions across different domains. PHP's ability to handle data processing, communication with IoT devices via MQTT, and web development makes it a valuable tool for building robust and scalable IoT applications. As the IoT ecosystem continues to grow, PHP's role in IoT solutions is expected to expand further, offering innovative solutions to a wide range of challenges.

Chapter 11: PHP 7 for Mobile App Development

Section 11.1: Basics of Mobile App Development with PHP

Mobile app development has become an integral part of the digital landscape, and PHP, known for its versatility, can be used effectively for creating mobile applications. In this section, we will explore the basics of mobile app development with PHP and understand how PHP can be leveraged for this purpose.

Introduction to Mobile App Development

Mobile app development refers to the process of creating software applications specifically designed to run on mobile devices such as smartphones and tablets. These applications can be developed for various platforms, including iOS (Apple), Android (Google), and Windows Mobile (Microsoft). Mobile apps offer a way to deliver content and services to users on the go, making them an essential part of modern business and technology.

Why Use PHP for Mobile App Development

PHP is traditionally associated with web development, but it can play a significant role in mobile app development too. Here are some reasons why PHP can be a valuable choice:

1. **Familiarity**: Many developers are already proficient in PHP, making it easier to transition to mobile app development.
2. **Cost-Efficiency**: PHP is open-source and free to use, reducing development costs compared to other languages.

3. **Server-Side Logic**: PHP can handle server-side logic for mobile apps, enabling real-time data processing and communication with databases.
4. **Cross-Platform Development**: PHP can be used for cross-platform mobile app development, reducing the need to write separate code for different platforms.
5. **Integration**: PHP can easily integrate with other technologies and APIs, making it versatile for mobile app functionality.

Building the Foundation

To get started with mobile app development in PHP, you'll need to set up a development environment that includes the necessary tools and libraries. This typically involves installing PHP, a web server, and a mobile app development framework or platform. Popular choices for mobile app development in PHP include using frameworks like Flutter, React Native, or building web-based mobile apps using PHP for the backend.

Key Concepts in Mobile App Development

Before diving into mobile app development with PHP, it's essential to grasp some key concepts:

1. **User Interface (UI)**: Designing an intuitive and responsive UI is crucial for a mobile app's success. PHP can be used to generate dynamic UI elements and templates.
2. **Backend Development**: PHP will primarily be used for backend development in mobile apps, handling tasks such as user authentication, data storage, and API integration.
3. **APIs**: Mobile apps often interact with external services and APIs. PHP can facilitate communication with these APIs

to fetch data and perform various functions.

4. **Security**: Mobile apps must be secure to protect user data. PHP offers robust security features, and developers should follow best practices to ensure app security.
5. **Testing**: Rigorous testing is essential to identify and fix bugs in mobile apps. Automated testing tools and frameworks can be integrated with PHP-based mobile app projects.

Conclusion

Mobile app development with PHP is a viable option for developers looking to leverage their PHP skills in the mobile app ecosystem. With the right tools, frameworks, and best practices, PHP can be a valuable asset for creating feature-rich and cross-platform mobile applications. In the upcoming sections, we will delve deeper into specific aspects of mobile app development with PHP, including API integration, cross-platform development, and performance optimization.

Section 11.2: APIs for Mobile Apps

In mobile app development, the integration of APIs (Application Programming Interfaces) is a common practice to enhance functionality and access external services. APIs act as intermediaries that allow your mobile app to communicate with web services, databases, and other resources. This section focuses on using APIs for mobile apps developed with PHP.

Why Use APIs in Mobile Apps

APIs serve several essential purposes in mobile app development:

1. **Access to External Services**: APIs enable your mobile app

to access external services and data, such as social media platforms, payment gateways, and mapping services.

2. **Data Retrieval**: APIs provide a way to fetch data from remote servers, making it possible to display real-time information to users.
3. **Authentication**: APIs often require authentication to ensure secure access, and they allow mobile apps to authenticate users with external services.
4. **Cross-Platform Compatibility**: APIs allow you to build cross-platform apps that can run on different operating systems while still accessing the same backend services.
5. **Scalability**: By relying on external APIs, your app can scale more easily as the backend infrastructure is managed by the API providers.

API Integration in PHP Mobile Apps

When developing mobile apps with PHP, integrating APIs can significantly enhance the app's functionality. Here are the key steps involved in API integration:

1. **Selecting the Right API**: Choose the API(s) that align with your app's objectives. Consider factors like documentation, ease of use, and pricing.
2. **Register for API Access**: Many APIs require developers to sign up for access. This often involves obtaining API keys or tokens, which are used for authentication.
3. **API Documentation**: Carefully review the API documentation provided by the service provider. This documentation outlines how to make requests, the required parameters, and the expected responses.
4. **HTTP Requests**: PHP can send HTTP requests (GET, POST, PUT, DELETE) to interact with APIs. Libraries

like cURL or Guzzle can simplify making these requests.

5. **Data Parsing**: Once data is received from the API, it needs to be parsed into a usable format. Common formats include JSON and XML, which can be processed with PHP's built-in functions.
6. **Error Handling**: Implement robust error handling to manage scenarios where API requests fail or return unexpected results. This ensures a seamless user experience.
7. **Testing**: Thoroughly test API integrations to ensure they work correctly. Pay attention to edge cases and handle potential errors gracefully.

Example: Fetching Weather Data

Let's consider a simple example of fetching weather data from a weather API in a PHP mobile app:

```
// Replace with your API key and endpoint

$apiKey = 'your_api_key';

$apiEndpoint = 'https://api.weather.com/data';

// Make a GET request to fetch weather data

$response =
file_get_contents("$apiEndpoint?city=NewYork&apiKey=$apiKey");

if ($response) {

$weatherData = json_decode($response, true);

if (isset($weatherData['temperature'])) {

echo "Current temperature in New York: " .
$weatherData['temperature'] . "°C";
```

```
} else {

echo "Failed to retrieve weather data.";

}

} else {

echo "API request failed.";

}
```

In this example, we retrieve weather data by sending a GET request to the weather API's endpoint. We handle the response, parse the JSON data, and display the current temperature.

Conclusion

API integration is a powerful tool in mobile app development with PHP. It enables your app to leverage external services and data, enhancing its capabilities and providing a better user experience. When implementing API integrations, it's essential to follow best practices, handle errors gracefully, and stay updated with any changes made by API providers to ensure your app's functionality remains intact. In the next section, we will explore the integration of PHP with Android and iOS, allowing us to create cross-platform mobile apps.

Section 11.3: Integrating PHP with Android and iOS

Integrating PHP with mobile app development extends beyond using APIs; it involves creating cross-platform mobile apps that utilize PHP for server-side functionality. In this section, we'll explore how to integrate PHP with both Android and iOS apps.

Android App Development with PHP

1. PHP as a Backend: In Android app development, PHP often plays the role of a server-side backend. You can create APIs or web services in PHP that your Android app interacts with. PHP frameworks like Laravel or Slim are commonly used to build such backends.

2. HTTP Requests: Android apps can make HTTP requests to PHP scripts using libraries like HttpURLConnection or OkHttp. These requests can send data, such as user input or device information, to the PHP backend for processing.

3. JSON Parsing: PHP backends typically respond with data in JSON format. Android apps can parse this JSON data to extract information that can be displayed to users or used within the app's logic.

Example: Making an HTTP Request in Android

```
import android.os.AsyncTask;

import java.io.BufferedReader;

import java.io.InputStreamReader;

import java.net.HttpURLConnection;

import java.net.URL;

public class FetchData extends AsyncTask<Void, Void, String> {

@Override

protected String doInBackground(Void... voids) {
```

```
try {
URL url = new URL("https://example.com/api/data.php");
HttpURLConnection conn = (HttpURLConnection) url.openConnection();
conn.setRequestMethod("GET");
BufferedReader reader = new BufferedReader(new InputStreamReader(conn.getInputStream()));
StringBuilder response = new StringBuilder();
String line;
while ((line = reader.readLine()) != null) {
response.append(line);
}
reader.close();
conn.disconnect();
return response.toString();
} catch (Exception e) {
e.printStackTrace();
return null;
}
}
@Override
```

```
protected void onPostExecute(String result) {
if (result != null) {
// Parse and use the JSON data here
} else {
// Handle errors
}
}
}
```

iOS App Development with PHP

1. PHP as a Backend: In iOS app development, PHP can also serve as a backend for handling data and business logic. You can create RESTful APIs using PHP frameworks like Symfony or Lumen, which iOS apps can interact with.

2. HTTP Requests: iOS apps can make HTTP requests to PHP endpoints using libraries like URLSession. These requests can be used for user authentication, data retrieval, or other interactions with the PHP backend.

3. JSON Parsing: As with Android, PHP typically responds with data in JSON format. iOS apps can parse this JSON data to work with the information provided by the PHP backend.

Example: Making an HTTP Request in iOS (Swift)

```
import Foundation
```

```
func fetchData() {
if let url = URL(string: "https://example.com/api/data.php") {
let task = URLSession.shared.dataTask(with: url) { data, response, error in
if let data = data {
do {
let json = try JSONSerialization.jsonObject(with: data, options: [])
// Process and use the JSON data here
} catch {
// Handle JSON parsing errors
}
} else if let error = error {
// Handle network errors
}
}
task.resume()
}
}
```

Conclusion

Integrating PHP with mobile app development allows you to leverage PHP's server-side capabilities to enhance the functionality of your Android and iOS apps. By creating APIs or web services with PHP, you can facilitate communication between your mobile apps and the server, enabling features such as user authentication, data retrieval, and real-time updates. Properly integrating PHP with mobile app development requires a good understanding of HTTP requests, data parsing, and error handling in both Android and iOS development environments. In the next section, we'll explore cross-platform development with PHP, which can streamline the process of building apps for multiple platforms.

Section 11.4: Cross-Platform Development with PHP

Cross-platform app development allows you to build mobile applications that can run on multiple operating systems, such as Android and iOS, using a single codebase. PHP can be utilized in various ways for cross-platform development, making it easier to maintain and update apps for different platforms simultaneously.

Using PHP for Backend Services

One common approach to cross-platform development is to use PHP as the backend server for your mobile apps. Regardless of whether you are developing for Android or iOS, the mobile app can communicate with the PHP backend using HTTP requests. The PHP backend can handle tasks like user authentication, data storage, and business logic. This approach streamlines development because you maintain a single codebase for the server-side logic.

Example: Cross-Platform App Architecture

```
+———————————+
```

| Cross-Platform |

| Mobile App |

+————————–+

|

+————————–+

| PHP |

| Backend |

+————————–+

|

+————————–+

| Database |

+————————–+

Cross-Platform Development Frameworks

Several cross-platform development frameworks allow you to create mobile apps using PHP and a single codebase. These frameworks facilitate the creation of native-like apps for both Android and iOS. Some popular options include:

1. Flutter: Flutter is a Google-developed open-source UI framework that allows you to build natively compiled applications for mobile, web, and desktop from a single codebase. While Flutter primarily uses Dart as its programming language, you can also integrate PHP for backend services.

2. React Native: React Native, developed by Facebook, enables you to create mobile applications using JavaScript and React. You can use PHP for backend development and API integration while building the frontend with React Native.

3. Apache Cordova (PhoneGap): Cordova is a platform for building native mobile applications using HTML, CSS, and JavaScript. You can incorporate PHP for backend services and use web technologies for the frontend.

Example of Cross-Platform App Development

Here's a simplified example of how PHP can be used in a cross-platform app development scenario:

1. **Backend Development**: Create a PHP backend that provides RESTful APIs for your mobile app. These APIs handle user registration, authentication, data retrieval, and any other server-side functionality.
2. **Frontend Development**: Develop the frontend of your cross-platform app using a framework like Flutter, React Native, or Cordova. Use HTTP requests to communicate with the PHP backend and fetch data.
3. **Authentication**: Implement user authentication on both Android and iOS by sending user credentials to the PHP backend. The backend validates the credentials and returns a token for subsequent API requests.

4. **Data Storage**: Store and retrieve data from the PHP backend using API endpoints. Both Android and iOS apps can use the same API calls to access the data.
5. **Push Notifications**: If your app requires push notifications, PHP can be used to send notifications to both Android and iOS devices through Firebase Cloud Messaging (FCM) or Apple Push Notification Service (APNs).

By adopting this approach, you can significantly reduce development time and effort while maintaining consistent functionality across different platforms. Cross-platform development with PHP offers a cost-effective and efficient solution for reaching a wider audience with your mobile applications.

In the next section, we'll explore performance optimization techniques specific to mobile app development with PHP.

Section 11.5: Performance Optimization for Mobile Apps

Mobile app performance is crucial for providing a smooth and responsive user experience. When developing mobile apps with PHP, it's essential to employ various optimization techniques to ensure that your app runs efficiently on both Android and iOS devices. In this section, we'll explore some performance optimization strategies specific to PHP-based mobile app development.

1. Caching: Implement caching mechanisms to reduce server load and minimize data transfer between the mobile app and the PHP backend. Use technologies like Memcached or Redis to store frequently accessed data, such as API responses,

database query results, and images.

```php
// Example PHP code for caching with Memcached

$memcached = new Memcached();

$memcached->addServer('localhost', 11211);

$key = 'cached_data';

$data = $memcached->get($key);

if ($data === false) {

// Fetch data from the database or API

$data = fetchDataFromDatabaseOrApi();

// Store the data in the cache for future use

$memcached->set($key, $data, 3600); // Cache for one hour

}

// Use the cached data

echo $data;
```

2. Optimized API Endpoints: Design your API endpoints to return only the necessary data and avoid over-fetching. Use pagination and filtering to limit the amount of data transmitted. Minimize the use of large payloads in API responses, especially for mobile networks.

3. Code Profiling: Profile your PHP code to identify performance bottlenecks. Tools like Xdebug and Blackfire Profiler can help pinpoint areas that require

optimization. Optimize database queries, reduce unnecessary function calls, and optimize loops.

```
// Example of code profiling with Xdebug

$xhprofData = xhprof_disable();

$XHProfRuns = new XHProfRuns_Default();

$runId = $XHProfRuns->save_run($xhprofData, 'myapp');
```

4. Image Compression: Compress images to reduce their file sizes before serving them to mobile devices. Use image optimization libraries or services to ensure that images are appropriately sized and formatted for mobile screens.

```
// Example of image compression using the GD library

$image = imagecreatefromjpeg('image.jpg');

imagejpeg($image, 'compressed_image.jpg', 80); // 80% quality
```

5. Minification and Bundling: Minify JavaScript and CSS files to reduce their size. Bundle multiple files into one to minimize the number of HTTP requests made by the mobile app. Tools like UglifyJS and CSS minifiers can help with this.

6. Lazy Loading: Implement lazy loading for resources such as images and videos. Load content only when it's visible to the user, reducing the initial load time of your mobile app.

```
<!—Example of lazy loading for images—>
```

```
<img src="placeholder.jpg" data-src="image.jpg" alt="Lazy-loaded image">
```

7. Background Processing: Offload resource-intensive tasks, such as image processing or data synchronization, to background processes. Use tools like Gearman or RabbitMQ to queue and process tasks asynchronously.

```
// Example of background processing with Gearman

$gmworker = new GearmanWorker();

$gmworker->addServer();

$gmworker->addFunction('process_image', 'processImageFunction');

while ($gmworker->work());
```

8. Network Optimization: Minimize the number of network requests made by your mobile app. Combine API requests, use HTTP/2 for faster loading, and enable GZIP compression on the server to reduce data transfer.

9. Resource Management: Manage memory and resources efficiently in your PHP code. Release unused resources, close database connections after use, and avoid memory leaks.

```
// Example of closing a database connection

$pdo = new PDO('mysql:host=localhost;dbname=mydb', 'username', 'password');

// ... perform database operations ...
```

$pdo = **null**; *// Close the database connection*

10. Testing and Profiling: Continuously test your mobile app's performance on real devices and use profiling tools to identify and address performance issues as they arise. Monitor server resource usage to ensure optimal performance.

By implementing these performance optimization techniques in your PHP-based mobile app development workflow, you can deliver faster, more responsive, and efficient applications for both Android and iOS platforms. Regularly review and update your app's performance strategies to keep up with changing user demands and hardware capabilities.

Chapter 12: Testing and Debugging in PHP 7

Section 12.1: Debugging Techniques in PHP

Debugging is an essential part of the software development process. It involves identifying and fixing issues or errors in your PHP code to ensure that your applications run smoothly. In this section, we'll explore various debugging techniques and tools available for PHP developers.

1. Print Statements:

One of the simplest debugging techniques is to use echo or print statements to print variable values, messages, or debug information to the screen or log files. This can help you understand the flow of your code and identify issues.

$variable = 42;

```
echo "The value of \$variable is: " . $variable;
```

2. var_dump():

The var_dump() function is a powerful tool for inspecting variables, arrays, and objects. It provides detailed information about the type and value of a variable, making it useful for understanding the structure of complex data.

```
$myArray = [1, 2, 3];

var_dump($myArray);
```

3. die() or exit():

You can use the die() or exit() function to halt the execution of your script at a specific point. This can be helpful for stopping the script to inspect variables or check the flow of your code.

```
$condition = false;

if (!$condition) {

die("Script execution halted due to a false condition.");

}
```

4. Debugging Extensions:

PHP has several debugging extensions that provide advanced debugging capabilities. Xdebug is one of the most popular extensions, offering features like step debugging, breakpoints, and code profiling. To use Xdebug, you need to install and configure it in your PHP environment.

5. Debugging IDEs:

Integrated Development Environments (IDEs) such as PhpStorm, Visual Studio Code, and NetBeans come with built-in debugging tools. They allow you to set breakpoints, inspect variables, and step through your code line by line. IDEs often integrate seamlessly with debugging extensions like Xdebug.

6. Error Reporting:

PHP provides various error reporting settings that can help you identify and handle errors effectively. You can configure error reporting levels using the error_reporting directive in your PHP configuration or by setting it dynamically within your code.

```
// Enable error reporting for all errors except notices

error_reporting(E_ALL & ~E_NOTICE);
```

7. Custom Logging:

Implement custom logging mechanisms to record errors and debug information. You can use libraries like Monolog or write custom log functions to log messages to files, databases, or external services.

```
use Monolog\Logger;

use Monolog\Handler\StreamHandler;

// Create a logger

$logger = new Logger('my_logger');

$logger->pushHandler(new StreamHandler('app.log', Logger::DEBUG));
```

```
// Log a message

$logger->info('This is an informational message.');
```

8. Error Handling:

Implement error handling strategies in your code, such as try-catch blocks for exceptions and error-handling functions for custom error handling. This allows you to gracefully handle errors and prevent them from crashing your application.

```
try {

// Code that may throw an exception

// ...

} catch (Exception $e) {

// Handle the exception

echo "An error occurred: " . $e->getMessage();

}
```

9. Testing Environments:

Set up separate testing and development environments to isolate issues and test changes before deploying to production. This ensures that debugging and testing don't affect the live application.

10. Code Reviews:

Collaborate with team members through code reviews. Fresh perspectives can help identify issues that may not be apparent during individual debugging efforts.

Debugging is a skill that improves with practice and experience. As a PHP developer, mastering debugging techniques and using the right tools will make your development process more efficient and your applications more reliable.

Section 12.2: Writing and Running Unit Tests

Unit testing is a crucial aspect of software development that involves testing individual components or units of code in isolation. In PHP, unit tests are commonly written for functions, methods, or classes to ensure that they work as expected. In this section, we'll explore how to write and run unit tests in PHP.

Writing Unit Tests

1. **Choose a Testing Framework**:

   PHP provides various testing frameworks, such as PHPUnit, Codeception, and PHPSpec. PHPUnit is one of the most popular choices for writing unit tests. You need to install PHPUnit using Composer or other package management tools.

   composer require—dev phpunit/phpunit

1. **Create a Test File**:

For each unit of code you want to test, create a corresponding test file. These files typically follow a naming convention like MyClassTest.php for a class named MyClass.

1. **Write Test Methods**:

In your test file, create methods that contain test cases. Test cases are functions that assert whether a specific behavior of your code works as expected. PHPUnit provides assertion methods like assertEquals, assertTrue, and assertEmpty to check conditions.

```
use PHPUnit\Framework\TestCase;

class MyMathTest extends TestCase {

public function testAddition() {

$result = MyMath::add(2, 3);

$this->assertEquals(5, $result);

}

}
```

1. **Run Tests**:

To execute your tests, run PHPUnit from the command line, specifying the test file or directory.

```
vendor/bin/phpunit MyMathTest.php
```

PHPUnit will discover and run your test methods, providing feedback on whether each test passed or failed.

Benefits of Unit Testing

Unit testing offers several benefits in PHP development:

- **Early Bug Detection**: Unit tests catch bugs and regressions early in the development process, reducing the cost of fixing issues later.

- **Documentation**: Unit tests serve as documentation for how your code is intended to work, making it easier for developers to understand and maintain the codebase.

- **Refactoring Safety**: When refactoring or making changes to your code, unit tests ensure that existing functionality remains intact. If a test fails, it signals that a change has caused an issue.

- **Collaboration**: Unit tests enable collaboration among team members. New developers can write tests to understand the behavior of existing code and make changes confidently.

- **Continuous Integration**: Automated testing with unit tests is a crucial part of continuous integration (CI) pipelines, ensuring that code changes are thoroughly tested before deployment.

Best Practices for Unit Testing

To get the most out of unit testing in PHP, consider these best practices:

- Write test cases for both expected and edge cases.
- Keep test methods focused on one specific behavior.
- Use meaningful test method names that describe the behavior being tested.
- Ensure that your tests are independent and don't rely on each other.
- Mock external dependencies and avoid making actual external calls (e.g., to databases or APIs) in unit tests.

Unit testing is an essential skill for any PHP developer. It not only improves the quality of your code but also contributes to a more robust and maintainable codebase. By following best practices and regularly running unit tests, you can ensure that your PHP applications are reliable and free from critical bugs.

Section 12.3: Integration Testing Strategies

Integration testing is an important aspect of the software testing process, where individual components of an application are combined and tested as a group to ensure that they work together correctly. In this section, we'll explore strategies and best practices for conducting integration testing in PHP.

The Purpose of Integration Testing

Integration testing aims to uncover issues that may arise when different components, modules, or services of an application interact with each other. It helps ensure that the integration points are functioning as expected and that data flows correctly between components.

Types of Integration Testing

Integration testing can be categorized into several types:

1. **Top-Down Integration Testing**: In this approach, testing starts from the top level of the application's hierarchy and gradually moves down. Test stubs or mocks are used for lower-level components that have not been implemented yet.
2. **Bottom-Up Integration Testing**: This strategy begins with testing the lowest-level components and progressively adds higher-level components. It is useful when critical core components need to be validated early.
3. **Big Bang Integration Testing**: In this approach, all components are integrated simultaneously, and testing is performed on the entire system. This method is often used when the project is near completion.
4. **Incremental Integration Testing**: Integration is performed incrementally, one component at a time. This method helps identify issues early and allows for more controlled testing.

Best Practices for Integration Testing

To effectively conduct integration testing in PHP, consider the following best practices:

1. **Identify Integration Points**: Clearly define the integration points in your application, including APIs, databases, external services, and communication channels.
2. **Isolate Components**: Isolate the components being tested from external dependencies, such as databases or external services. Use mocks or stubs to simulate these dependencies.

3. **Testing Environment**: Maintain a separate testing environment that closely resembles the production environment. This ensures that integration tests mimic real-world scenarios.
4. **Test Data**: Use consistent and realistic test data. Ensure that data is set up and cleaned up correctly during integration tests.
5. **Automation**: Automate integration tests to run them consistently and frequently. Tools like PHPUnit can be used for integration testing in PHP.
6. **Logging and Monitoring**: Implement logging and monitoring to capture information about integration test runs and identify any failures or issues.

Integration Testing in PHP

In PHP, integration testing often involves testing the interaction between various components of a web application, such as the database, web server, and external APIs. PHPUnit, a popular testing framework, can be used for integration testing by creating test cases that exercise these interactions.

Here's a simplified example of an integration test for a PHP application that interacts with a MySQL database:

```
use PHPUnit\Framework\TestCase;

class DatabaseIntegrationTest extends TestCase {

protected $db;

protected function setUp(): void {

// Initialize the database connection
```

```
$this->db = new PDO('mysql:host=localhost;dbname=myapp', 'username', 'password');

}

public function testDatabaseConnection() {

// Check if the database connection is established

$this->assertInstanceOf(PDO::class, $this->db);

}

public function testUserDataRetrieval() {

// Query the database and assert the results

$stmt = $this->db->prepare('SELECT * FROM users WHERE id = ?');

$stmt->execute([1]);

$user = $stmt->fetch(PDO::FETCH_ASSOC);

$this->assertEquals('John Doe', $user['name']);

}

}
```

In this example, the DatabaseIntegrationTest class sets up a database connection in the setUp method and then defines test methods to check the database connection and retrieve user data.

Integration testing in PHP can become more complex depending on the application's architecture and integration points. However, following best practices and using appropriate testing tools will help you ensure the reliability and functionality of your integrated components.

Section 12.4: Performance Testing in PHP

Performance testing is a critical aspect of ensuring that a PHP application can handle the expected load and perform efficiently. In this section, we'll delve into performance testing strategies and tools in PHP.

The Importance of Performance Testing

Performance testing helps identify bottlenecks and performance-related issues in your PHP application. It ensures that the application can deliver a satisfactory user experience even under high load conditions. Common performance-related problems include slow response times, high resource consumption, and scalability limitations.

Types of Performance Testing

There are several types of performance testing, each focusing on specific aspects of an application's performance:

1. **Load Testing**: Load testing assesses how the application performs under a specific load, such as a certain number of concurrent users or requests. It helps determine if the application can handle expected traffic.
2. **Stress Testing**: Stress testing pushes the application beyond its intended capacity to identify failure points, such as when server resources are exhausted or response times become unacceptable.
3. **Scalability Testing**: Scalability testing evaluates how well the application can scale horizontally or vertically to

accommodate increased loads. It ensures that additional resources can be added when needed.

4. **Endurance Testing**: Endurance testing assesses the application's stability over an extended period. It helps identify memory leaks or resource depletion that may occur over time.

Performance Testing Tools in PHP

PHP offers several tools and libraries for conducting performance tests. Here are some notable options:

1. **Apache JMeter**: Although primarily designed for Java applications, Apache JMeter can be used to test PHP applications. It supports various load testing scenarios and can simulate a large number of concurrent users.
2. **ab (Apache Benchmark)**: ab is a command-line tool that comes with the Apache HTTP Server. It is simple to use and can be used to send a high number of requests to a PHP script to measure its performance.
3. **Siege**: Siege is another command-line tool for load testing web applications. It allows you to define scenarios and simulate multiple users accessing your PHP application simultaneously.
4. **Xdebug**: Xdebug is a PHP extension that provides profiling and tracing capabilities. It can help identify performance bottlenecks in your PHP code by generating profiling reports.

Conducting Performance Tests

To perform performance testing in PHP, you'll need to follow these general steps:

1. **Define Performance Goals**: Determine the specific performance criteria you want to test, such as response time, throughput, or resource utilization.
2. **Identify Test Scenarios**: Create test scenarios that represent real-world usage patterns. This may include user registration, login, database queries, or API requests.
3. **Select the Right Tool**: Choose a performance testing tool that suits your requirements and budget. Tools like Apache JMeter are suitable for complex load testing, while ab and Siege are more straightforward.
4. **Execute Tests**: Run your performance tests with various configurations, gradually increasing the load to observe how your PHP application behaves.
5. **Analyze Results**: Analyze the test results to identify bottlenecks or performance issues. Look for slow queries, excessive memory usage, or other anomalies.
6. **Optimize and Retest**: Once issues are identified, make optimizations to your PHP code, database queries, or server configurations. Then, retest to ensure improvements have been made.

Performance testing should be an iterative process, and it's essential to conduct tests regularly, especially when making significant changes to your application. By doing so, you can ensure that your PHP application meets performance expectations and provides a responsive user experience.

Section 12.5: Using Debugging Tools and IDEs

Debugging is an essential part of software development, and in PHP, there are various debugging tools and integrated development environments (IDEs) that can significantly streamline the debugging process. In this section, we'll explore some of the popular tools and techniques for debugging PHP code.

Built-in PHP Debugging Functions

PHP provides a set of built-in functions for debugging that can be helpful during development. These functions allow you to print variables, inspect code execution, and trace program flow:

1. echo and var_dump(): These functions are simple yet effective for printing variable values and data structures to the browser or console. They are handy for quickly inspecting variables and their contents.

```
$name = "John";

echo "Hello, " . $name;

var_dump($name);
```

1. print_r(): Similar to var_dump(), print_r() is used for displaying the structure of arrays and objects in a more human-readable format.

```
$fruits = ["apple", "banana", "cherry"];

print_r($fruits);
```

1. die() and exit(): These functions allow you to terminate script execution at a specific point and display a custom message. They are useful for stopping code execution to inspect variables or troubleshoot issues.

```
$value = 42;
```

```
if ($value > 50) {

echo "Value is greater than 50.";

} else {

die("Value is not greater than 50.");

}
```

PHP Debugging Tools and IDEs

While the built-in debugging functions can be helpful, dedicated debugging tools and IDEs offer more advanced features and a smoother debugging experience:

1. **Xdebug**: Xdebug is a powerful PHP extension that provides extensive debugging capabilities. It allows you to set breakpoints, step through code, inspect variables, and profile your code's performance. Xdebug integrates with IDEs like PhpStorm, Visual Studio Code, and Eclipse PDT.
2. **PhpStorm**: PhpStorm is a popular PHP-focused integrated development environment by JetBrains. It offers robust debugging features, including Xdebug integration, code navigation, and advanced code analysis. PhpStorm also supports other web technologies, making it a comprehensive solution for PHP development.
3. **Visual Studio Code (VS Code)**: VS Code is a lightweight, open-source code editor developed by Microsoft. It has a rich ecosystem of extensions, including PHP debugging extensions like PHP Debug and Xdebug. VS Code's debugging features provide an excellent debugging experience for PHP developers.

4. **Eclipse PDT**: Eclipse PHP Development Tools (PDT) is an open-source IDE tailored for PHP development. It offers debugging capabilities with Xdebug integration, code completion, and project management features.
5. **NetBeans**: NetBeans is another open-source IDE that supports PHP development. It provides a user-friendly interface for debugging PHP applications, making it suitable for developers who prefer an all-in-one development environment.

Debugging Best Practices

Regardless of the debugging tool or IDE you choose, here are some best practices for effective debugging:

• **Use Version Control**: Always work with version control systems like Git to track changes in your code. This allows you to revert to a known working state if debugging becomes challenging.

• **Write Test Cases**: Implement unit tests and integration tests to catch issues early in the development process. Debugging becomes more manageable when you have a suite of tests that validate your code's behavior.

• **Set Clear Objectives**: Before debugging, define clear objectives and hypotheses about the issue. Knowing what you're looking for can help you narrow down the problem more efficiently.

• **Use Logging**: Implement logging mechanisms in your PHP application to record important information, errors, and debug messages. Log files can provide valuable insights into issues, especially in production environments.

- **Collaborate**: When debugging complex issues, don't hesitate to seek assistance from colleagues or online developer communities. Fresh perspectives and shared experiences can be invaluable.

Debugging is an essential skill for PHP developers, and mastering debugging tools and techniques can save you time and frustration during the development process. Whether you rely on built-in PHP functions or use dedicated debugging tools and IDEs, effective debugging practices are crucial for delivering high-quality PHP applications.

Chapter 13: PHP 7 and Social Media Integration

Section 13.1: Integrating Social Media APIs

In today's interconnected world, social media integration is a crucial aspect of web development. It allows websites and applications to interact with popular social media platforms such as Facebook, Twitter, Instagram, and LinkedIn. In this section, we'll explore how to integrate social media APIs into your PHP applications to leverage the power of social sharing, authentication, and data access.

Why Social Media Integration?

Social media integration offers several benefits for web applications:

1. **User Engagement**: Users can easily share content from your website on their social media profiles, increasing your site's visibility and driving more traffic.
2. **Single Sign-On (SSO)**: Integrating social media authentication allows users to log in using their existing social media accounts, simplifying the registration and login process.
3. **Access to Social Data**: You can access user data from social media platforms (with user consent) to personalize content and user experiences.
4. **Social Sharing**: Implementing social sharing buttons enables users to share content with a single click, promoting your content virally.

Integrating Social Media APIs

To integrate social media platforms into your PHP application, you'll need to work with their respective APIs. Here's a high-level overview of the integration process:

1. **Create Developer Accounts**: To access social media APIs, you need developer accounts with the platforms you want to integrate. Visit the developer portals of platforms like Facebook for Developers, Twitter Developer Platform, or Google Developers Console to create your app.
2. **Obtain API Keys**: Once you've registered your app, you'll receive API keys and credentials (such as client IDs and secrets) that allow your application to communicate with the social media platforms.
3. **Choose an API Library**: PHP offers several libraries and SDKs for social media integration, making it easier to work with different APIs. Popular choices include the Facebook PHP SDK, TwitterOAuth, and Google APIs Client Library for PHP.
4. **Authentication**: Implement OAuth 2.0 or OAuth 1.0a authentication to allow users to grant your application access to their social media accounts. Users will be redirected to the social media platform's login page for authorization.

```
// Example using OAuth 2.0 with Facebook PHP SDK

$fb = new Facebook\Facebook([

'app_id' => 'YOUR_APP_ID',

'app_secret' => 'YOUR_APP_SECRET',
```

```
'default_graph_version' => 'v13.0',

]);

$helper = $fb->getRedirectLoginHelper();

$loginUrl =
$helper->getLoginUrl('https://your-app.com/
fb-callback.php', ['email', 'user_friends']);
```

1. **Access User Data**: Once authorized, your application can access user data, such as profile information, posts, photos, and friends. Make API requests to retrieve this data and use it in your application.

```
// Example using Facebook Graph API

try {

$response = $fb->get('/me?fields=id,name,email',
$accessToken);

$user = $response->getGraphUser();

} catch (Facebook\Exceptions\
FacebookResponseException $e) {

// Handle API errors

}
```

1. **Implement Social Sharing**: To enable social sharing, create share buttons that trigger API requests to post content on the user's social media profile. Provide user-friendly sharing options and pre-populate content for sharing.

```
// Example sharing a link using Facebook PHP SDK

$linkData = [

'link' => 'https://your-app.com/page-to-share.php',

'message' => 'Check out this amazing page!',

];

try {

$response = $fb->post('/me/feed', $linkData, $accessToken);

} catch (Facebook\Exceptions\FacebookResponseException $e) {

// Handle API errors

}
```

Challenges and Considerations

While social media integration offers numerous advantages, it also comes with challenges and considerations:

- **Privacy and Data Protection**: Ensure compliance with data protection regulations (e.g., GDPR) and respect user privacy when handling their data from social media platforms.
- **Rate Limiting**: Be aware of rate limits imposed by social media APIs to avoid excessive requests and service disruptions.

- **Maintenance**: APIs and SDKs may change over time, requiring periodic updates to your integration code.

- **Security**: Protect API keys and credentials, and implement secure authentication mechanisms to prevent unauthorized access.

- **User Experience**: Provide a seamless user experience during the authentication process to minimize friction for users.

Integrating social media APIs can enhance your PHP applications by connecting them to the vast social networks where users spend their time. Whether it's sharing content, authenticating users, or accessing social data, these integrations can open up new opportunities for engagement and growth.

Section 13.2: Building Social Networking Features

In this section, we'll delve into building social networking features within your PHP web application. Social networking features allow users to connect, communicate, and interact with each other on your platform. These features can include friend requests, user profiles, comments, likes, and messaging systems. By implementing these elements, you can create a more engaging and interactive community for your users.

User Profiles

User profiles are a fundamental part of any social networking platform. Each user should have a profile page where they can showcase information about themselves, such as their profile picture, bio, and recent activity. Here's how you can create user profiles in PHP:

1. **User Registration**: Implement user registration and login functionality to allow users to create accounts and log in.
2. **Profile Information**: Create a database table to store user profiles, including fields for profile pictures, bios, and other relevant details.
3. **Profile Pages**: Develop individual profile pages for users that display their information. You can use PHP templates to generate these pages dynamically based on the user's ID.
4. **Privacy Settings**: Allow users to set privacy preferences for their profiles, deciding who can view their information and activity.

Friend Requests

Friend requests are a common social networking feature that enables users to connect with each other. Here's how you can implement friend requests in PHP:

1. **Friendship Table**: Create a database table to store friend relationships. Each row should represent a friend connection between two users.
2. **Friend Requests**: Allow users to send friend requests to others. When a user sends a request, a notification is generated for the recipient.
3. **Accepting Requests**: Implement a mechanism for users to accept or decline friend requests. If accepted, the friend relationship is established in the database.
4. **Display Friends**: On user profiles, display the list of a user's friends, and provide options for removing friends if desired.

Comments and Likes

Comments and likes are essential for engaging discussions on social networking platforms. Users can comment on posts, photos, or other content, and they can also express their approval through likes. Here's how to implement these features:

1. **Database Structure**: Create tables to store comments and likes associated with specific posts or content.
2. **Commenting**: Allow users to add comments to posts. Each comment should be associated with the user who posted it, the content it relates to, and a timestamp.
3. **Liking**: Implement a "like" feature that lets users express their approval of content. Store these likes in a separate database table, linking them to the content and the user who liked it.
4. **Displaying Comments and Likes**: On content pages, display comments and the number of likes. Users can click to see all comments and who has liked the content.

Messaging Systems

Messaging systems enable private communication between users. Implementing a messaging system in PHP involves the following steps:

1. **Conversations**: Create a database structure to store conversations between users. Each conversation can have multiple messages.
2. **Message Sending**: Allow users to send messages to each other within the platform. Messages should be associated with the conversation they belong to.
3. **Notifications**: Implement real-time or email notifications for new messages to ensure users are aware of incoming

messages.

4. **Message History**: Provide users with a history of their conversations, making it easy to find and continue discussions.

By incorporating these social networking features into your PHP application, you can foster user engagement and create a vibrant online community. Keep in mind that these features require careful consideration of user privacy and security, as well as efficient database management to handle large volumes of user-generated content.

Section 13.3: Authentication with Social Media Platforms

Integrating authentication with social media platforms is a crucial aspect of many web applications. It allows users to log in or sign up using their existing social media accounts, simplifying the registration process and providing a convenient way to access your platform. In this section, we'll explore how to implement social media authentication in your PHP application.

Why Social Media Authentication?

1. **User Convenience**: Social media authentication eliminates the need for users to create yet another username and password. They can use their existing social media credentials, which is more convenient.
2. **Trust and Security**: Users may trust social media platforms more when it comes to authentication and data protection, making them more likely to use your service.
3. **Access to User Data**: Integrating with social media platforms can provide your application with access to user

data, such as their profile picture and email address (subject to user permissions), which can enhance user profiles and engagement.

Implementing Social Media Authentication

To implement social media authentication in your PHP application, follow these general steps:

1. **Choose Social Media Providers**: Decide which social media platforms you want to integrate with (e.g., Facebook, Google, Twitter).
2. **Create Developer Accounts**: Register as a developer on the chosen social media platforms to obtain API keys and credentials.
3. **Install OAuth Libraries**: PHP has various OAuth libraries that simplify the authentication process. You can choose libraries like OAuth 2.0 or third-party libraries like HybridAuth to handle authentication.
4. **Configure OAuth Settings**: Set up your OAuth credentials in your PHP application. This typically includes specifying the client ID and client secret provided by the social media platforms.
5. **Implement OAuth Flow**: Create the authentication flow in your application. This involves redirecting users to the social media platform's authentication page, where they can grant permission for your app to access their data.
6. **Handle Callbacks**: After users authenticate, they are redirected back to your application with an access token. Implement the callback handler to process this token and retrieve user information.
7. **Create User Accounts**: If it's a new user, create an account in your database using the obtained user data. If it's an

existing user, log them in.

8. **Manage Permissions**: Ensure you request the necessary permissions from users to access their data. Respect user privacy settings and comply with data protection regulations.

Example Code (OAuth with Facebook)

Here's a simplified example of how you can use the OAuth library to integrate Facebook authentication into your PHP application:

```
// Include the OAuth library

require 'oauth.php';

// Facebook OAuth credentials

$clientId = 'your_client_id';

$clientSecret = 'your_client_secret';

$redirectUri = 'https://yourapp.com/callback.php';

// Initialize the OAuth client

$oauth = new OAuth($clientId, $clientSecret, $redirectUri);

// Redirect users to Facebook for authentication

$oauth->redirectToProvider('facebook');
```

In the above code, replace 'your_client_id' and 'your_client_secret' with your Facebook app's credentials. After the user authenticates, they will be redirected to the callback URL where you can handle the token and create or log in the user.

Remember to follow the documentation of your chosen OAuth library and the specific social media platform for detailed integration instructions.

By implementing social media authentication, you can enhance user onboarding and simplify the login process while also gaining access to valuable user data to personalize their experience on your platform.

Section 13.4: Social Media Data Analysis

Once you have successfully integrated social media authentication into your PHP application, you can take advantage of the wealth of data available from these platforms. Social media data analysis is a powerful tool for understanding user behavior, improving engagement, and making informed decisions about your application's features and content. In this section, we'll explore how to perform social media data analysis in PHP.

Types of Social Media Data

Social media platforms offer various types of data that can be analyzed:

1. **User Profiles**: Information like user names, profile pictures, and email addresses (subject to user permissions) can enhance user profiles on your platform.
2. **User Activity**: Data on what users do on your platform, such as likes, comments, and shares, can help you understand their preferences.
3. **Demographics**: Social media platforms often provide data on user demographics like age, location, and interests, allowing you to target specific user groups.

4. **Engagement Metrics**: Metrics like engagement rate, click-through rate, and conversion rate help evaluate the success of your social media campaigns.
5. **Sentiment Analysis**: Analyzing user-generated content for sentiment (positive, negative, neutral) can help gauge public opinion about your brand or products.

Using PHP for Social Media Data Analysis

To perform social media data analysis in PHP, follow these steps:

1. **Data Retrieval**: Use API endpoints provided by the social media platform to retrieve the desired data. You'll need to authenticate with the platform using the access token obtained during authentication.
2. **Data Parsing**: Parse the data returned by the API. Most APIs provide data in JSON format, which you can easily decode in PHP using functions like json_decode().
3. **Data Storage**: Store the retrieved data in your application's database for analysis. Ensure that your database schema is designed to accommodate the specific data you need.
4. **Data Analysis**: Implement algorithms or use libraries in PHP for data analysis. For example, you can calculate engagement rates, perform sentiment analysis, or generate user behavior patterns.

Example Code (Twitter Data Retrieval)

Here's a simplified example of how to retrieve user tweets from Twitter using the Twitter API and PHP:

```
// Include TwitterOAuth library

require 'twitteroauth/autoload.php';
```

```
use Abraham\TwitterOAuth\TwitterOAuth;

// Twitter API credentials

$consumerKey = 'your_consumer_key';

$consumerSecret = 'your_consumer_secret';

$accessToken = 'user_access_token';

$accessTokenSecret = 'user_access_token_secret';

// Initialize TwitterOAuth

$connection = new TwitterOAuth($consumerKey, $consumerSecret, $accessToken, $accessTokenSecret);

// Retrieve user's tweets

$tweets = $connection->get("statuses/user_timeline", ["count" => 10]);

// Parse and display tweets

foreach ($tweets as $tweet) {

echo $tweet->text . "<br>";

}
```

In this example, replace 'your_consumer_key', 'your_consumer_secret', 'user_access_token', and 'user_access_token_secret' with your Twitter API credentials. This code retrieves and displays the latest 10 tweets from the authenticated user.

Remember that each social media platform has its own API and data retrieval methods, so consult their documentation for specific details.

Social media data analysis can provide valuable insights into user behavior, trends, and preferences, helping you make data-driven decisions to improve your application's performance and user experience.

Section 13.5: Case Studies: Social Media Campaigns with PHP

In this section, we'll explore real-world case studies of successful social media campaigns that utilized PHP to achieve their goals. These campaigns demonstrate how PHP can be a powerful tool for enhancing engagement, reaching a wider audience, and achieving various marketing objectives.

Case Study 1: Facebook Campaign for User Acquisition

Objective:

A mobile app startup aimed to acquire more users for its fitness tracking app. They decided to run a user acquisition campaign on Facebook.

Implementation:

1. **Ad Campaign**: The startup created engaging ad creatives showcasing the app's features and benefits. They used Facebook Ads Manager to target specific demographics, interests, and behaviors relevant to fitness enthusiasts.

2. **Landing Page**: Clicking on the ads led users to a PHP-powered landing page. This page provided detailed information about the app, user testimonials, and a download button.
3. **User Registration**: Users who clicked the download button were redirected to the app store. After installing the app, they were prompted to register using their email or social media accounts, which were integrated using PHP OAuth libraries.
4. **Analytics**: The startup implemented PHP-based analytics to track user engagement, including app installations, registrations, and in-app activities.

Results:

- The campaign resulted in a significant increase in app installations.

- PHP-based analytics helped the startup understand user behavior and optimize the app for better user retention.

Case Study 2: Twitter Contest for Brand Promotion

Objective:

A well-established clothing brand wanted to promote its new collection and engage with its Twitter followers.

Implementation:

1. **Contest Concept**: The brand decided to run a Twitter contest where participants could submit photos of

themselves wearing the brand's clothing.

2. **PHP Backend**: They developed a PHP backend that collected and stored contest entries in a database. PHP was used to ensure data security and validation.
3. **Hashtag Integration**: Participants were required to use a specific contest hashtag in their tweets. PHP code periodically searched Twitter for tweets with the hashtag, fetching and displaying them on the contest website in real-time.
4. **Voting Mechanism**: PHP was used to create a voting mechanism where users could vote for their favorite contest entries. The backend ensured fair and secure voting.

Results:

- The contest generated a buzz on Twitter, resulting in increased brand mentions and engagement.
- PHP-driven real-time updates on the contest website kept participants engaged throughout the campaign.

Case Study 3: Instagram Influencer Marketing with PHP

Objective:

An e-commerce business wanted to leverage Instagram influencer marketing to increase product sales.

Implementation:

1. **Influencer Selection**: The business identified relevant

Instagram influencers and collaborated with them to promote their products.

2. **PHP-based Tracking**: PHP was used to create a unique tracking link for each influencer. When followers clicked on these links and made purchases, the PHP backend recorded the sales and attributed them to the respective influencer.
3. **Payment Automation**: PHP scripts automatically calculated influencer commissions based on sales attributed to them. Payments were processed securely through PHP-integrated payment gateways.
4. **Reporting**: Influencers and the business had access to real-time reports on sales, commissions, and campaign performance, all powered by PHP.

Results:

- The influencer marketing campaign led to a significant increase in product sales.

- PHP automation streamlined commission calculations and payments, simplifying the campaign management process.

These case studies highlight how PHP can be effectively used in various social media campaigns, from user acquisition to influencer marketing. PHP's versatility, coupled with its robust libraries and frameworks, makes it a valuable tool for marketers and businesses aiming to succeed in the ever-evolving world of social media marketing.

Chapter 14: PHP 7 in E-commerce

Section 14.1: Building an E-commerce Website with PHP

In this section, we'll delve into the essential aspects of building a robust e-commerce website using PHP. E-commerce has witnessed significant growth in recent years, and PHP is a popular choice for developing feature-rich online stores. We'll explore key considerations, best practices, and sample code snippets for creating a successful e-commerce platform.

Understanding E-commerce Requirements

Before diving into development, it's crucial to understand the specific requirements of your e-commerce website. Consider factors like the type of products you'll sell, payment gateways you'll integrate, and the scale of your operation. This initial planning phase will guide your development process.

Setting Up the Development Environment

To get started, ensure you have a suitable development environment with PHP, a web server (such as Apache or Nginx), and a database system (like MySQL or PostgreSQL) installed. Tools like XAMPP or WAMP can provide a preconfigured environment for local development.

Choosing an E-commerce Framework

Selecting the right PHP framework can significantly simplify e-commerce development. Popular options include:

- **Magento**: A powerful and feature-rich e-commerce platform.
- **WooCommerce**: A WordPress plugin for building online stores.
- **OpenCart**: A user-friendly and customizable e-commerce solution.
- **Symfony with Sylius**: A flexible and extendable framework for e-commerce.

Creating Product Listings

To display products on your website, you'll need a database to store product information and images. Use SQL queries or an ORM (Object-Relational Mapping) like Doctrine in Symfony to interact with the database. Create a user-friendly interface for managing product listings.

Implementing Shopping Cart Functionality

Building a shopping cart is a critical component of any e-commerce website. Design and develop a cart system that allows users to add and remove items, update quantities, and calculate totals. Ensure data security and validation to prevent fraudulent activities.

Integrating Payment Gateways

Integrate payment gateways like PayPal, Stripe, or Authorize.Net to facilitate secure transactions. Most payment gateways provide APIs and PHP SDKs for seamless integration. Implement server-side validation of payment responses to ensure accuracy and security.

Managing User Accounts

Implement user authentication and account management features. Users should be able to create accounts, log in, reset passwords, and update their profiles. Store user data securely and hash passwords to protect user information.

Handling Orders and Inventory

Develop a system to manage orders, including order processing, invoicing, and order status tracking. Implement inventory management to update product availability based on orders placed.

Ensuring Security

Security is paramount in e-commerce. Implement security measures like HTTPS, data encryption, and input validation to protect user data. Regularly update and patch your software to address security vulnerabilities.

Implementing Search and Filters

Enhance the shopping experience by implementing search functionality and product filters. Use PHP libraries like Elasticsearch or integrate with search engines like Solr for efficient search capabilities.

Optimizing Performance

Optimize your e-commerce website for speed and scalability. Use caching mechanisms, CDNs (Content Delivery Networks), and database indexing to reduce page load times. Monitor server performance and scale resources as needed.

In this section, we've covered the initial steps for building an e-commerce website with PHP. Keep in mind that e-commerce development is an ongoing process, requiring continuous improvements, security updates, and feature enhancements to meet the evolving needs of your customers and business.

Section 14.2: Payment Gateway Integration

Payment gateway integration is a crucial aspect of any e-commerce website. It allows your customers to make secure online transactions, and as a PHP developer, you'll need to implement this feature effectively. In this section, we'll explore the steps involved in integrating payment gateways into your PHP-based e-commerce platform.

Understanding Payment Gateway Integration

A payment gateway is a service that handles the online payment process, securely transferring payment data between the customer, your website, and the payment processor. Common payment gateways include PayPal, Stripe, Authorize.Net, and more. Here's a simplified overview of how payment gateway integration works:

1. **Customer Initiates Payment**: When a customer decides to make a purchase on your website, they choose a payment method (e.g., credit card, PayPal).
2. **Data Encryption**: The customer's payment data, such as credit card details, is securely encrypted on the client-side using SSL/TLS (Secure Sockets Layer/Transport Layer Security) to protect it during transmission.

3. **Payment Request**: Your website sends a payment request with the encrypted data to the chosen payment gateway.
4. **Payment Processing**: The payment gateway receives the request, decrypts the data, and processes the payment. This may involve communication with the customer's bank to authorize the transaction.
5. **Transaction Result**: The payment gateway provides a response to your website, indicating whether the payment was successful or not.
6. **Order Confirmation**: Based on the response, your website updates the order status, sends a confirmation email to the customer, and completes the purchase.

Integration Options

Payment gateway integration can be done in several ways, depending on the payment gateway provider and your website's requirements. Here are some common integration options:

- **Hosted Payment Pages**: Some gateways offer hosted payment pages where customers are redirected to the gateway's secure page for payment processing. After completing the payment, customers are redirected back to your website.

- **Direct API Integration**: This approach allows you to handle the payment process entirely within your website. You collect and securely transmit payment data to the gateway using the payment gateway's API.

- **JavaScript Libraries**: Some gateways provide JavaScript libraries that help in creating custom payment forms and handling tokenization of payment data for added security.

Steps for Payment Gateway Integration

1. **Choose a Payment Gateway**: Select a payment gateway that suits your business needs and customer preferences. Ensure it supports PHP integration.
2. **Sign Up and Get API Credentials**: Create an account with the chosen payment gateway provider and obtain API credentials (usually API keys or tokens) required for integration.
3. **Install SDK or Library**: If the payment gateway offers an SDK or PHP library, download and install it in your project. This library simplifies communication with the gateway's API.
4. **Configure API Credentials**: Set up the API credentials in your PHP code, typically in a configuration file, to establish a secure connection with the gateway.
5. **Create Payment Forms**: Design and implement payment forms that collect necessary payment information from customers. Ensure that these forms are secure and compliant with Payment Card Industry Data Security Standard (PCI DSS) requirements.
6. **Tokenization (Optional)**: For added security, consider tokenizing payment data. Tokenization replaces sensitive data with a unique identifier (token) to reduce the risk of data breaches.
7. **Handle Responses**: Implement code to handle responses from the payment gateway. This includes processing successful payments and handling failed or declined transactions.
8. **Test Transactions**: Before deploying to a production environment, thoroughly test payment transactions using the gateway's sandbox or testing environment.

9. **Implement Error Handling**: Create error-handling mechanisms to deal with any unexpected issues during payment processing.
10. **Security Measures**: Ensure that your integration follows best practices for security, including data encryption, input validation, and protection against common vulnerabilities like SQL injection and cross-site scripting (XSS).
11. **Monitoring and Logging**: Implement logging and monitoring to track payment transactions and identify any issues or anomalies.
12. **Go Live**: Once testing is successful and you're confident in your integration, switch to the production environment of the payment gateway and start accepting real payments.

Remember that payment gateway integration requires careful consideration of security, compliance, and error handling. It's essential to stay up to date with any changes in the payment gateway's API and maintain your integration to provide a smooth and secure shopping experience for your customers.

Section 14.3: Shopping Cart Implementation

Implementing a shopping cart is a fundamental component of any e-commerce website. It allows customers to select and store items they want to purchase until they are ready to check out. In this section, we will discuss the essential steps to implement a shopping cart in your PHP-based e-commerce platform.

Understanding the Shopping Cart

A shopping cart serves as a virtual container that holds the selected products or items a customer intends to buy. It provides a way to manage the items, update quantities, remove products, and calculate the total cost of the order. Here are some key aspects of a shopping cart:

1. **Adding Items**: Customers can add products to the cart by clicking an "Add to Cart" button on a product page.
2. **Viewing Cart**: Shoppers can view the contents of their cart at any time during their shopping session.
3. **Modifying Cart**: Customers can change quantities, remove items, or even save items for later.
4. **Checkout**: When customers are ready to complete their purchase, they proceed to the checkout process.

Steps for Shopping Cart Implementation

1. Data Structure

To implement a shopping cart, you need to decide how to store cart data. Common options include session variables, cookies, or a database. Session variables are often used for temporary storage, while a database is suitable for persistent carts.

2. Add to Cart

When a customer clicks the "Add to Cart" button on a product page, you should capture the product's ID and quantity. You then add this information to the cart data structure.

```
// Sample code to add an item to the cart

$product_id = 123; // Product ID

$quantity = 2; // Quantity selected by the customer

// Check if the product is already in the cart
```

```
if (isset($_SESSION['cart'][$product_id])) {
// Increment the quantity if the product is already in the cart
$_SESSION['cart'][$product_id] += $quantity;
} else {
// Add the product to the cart if it's not already there
$_SESSION['cart'][$product_id] = $quantity;
}
```

3. View Cart

Create a page where customers can view the contents of their cart. Iterate through the cart data and display each product's details, including name, price, quantity, and subtotal. Provide options for customers to update quantities or remove items.

4. Modify Cart

Allow customers to modify their cart by changing the quantity of items or removing products. Make sure to update the cart data accordingly.

5. Calculate Total

Calculate the total cost of the order by summing up the subtotals of all items in the cart.

```
$total = 0;
foreach ($_SESSION['cart'] as $product_id => $quantity) {
```

```
// Fetch product details (e.g., price) from your database
$product_price = getProductPrice($product_id);
// Calculate subtotal for each item
$subtotal = $product_price * $quantity;
// Add subtotal to the total
$total += $subtotal;
}
```

6. Checkout Process

Implement a checkout process that guides customers through providing shipping information, selecting payment methods, and confirming their order. This may involve payment gateway integration, as discussed in the previous section (Section 14.2).

7. Persistence

If you want customers to be able to retrieve their cart contents even after they leave and return to your website, consider persisting cart data in a database and associating it with a user account.

8. Security

Ensure the security of your shopping cart, especially if it involves sensitive customer information or payment details. Use HTTPS to encrypt data transmission, sanitize user inputs, and implement authentication and authorization mechanisms.

9. Testing

Thoroughly test your shopping cart functionality, including edge cases, to ensure a seamless and error-free shopping experience for your customers.

Implementing a shopping cart is a critical component of e-commerce websites. It helps improve the user experience and can significantly impact conversion rates and sales. Careful planning and development are essential to create a reliable and user-friendly shopping cart system.

Section 14.4: Security in Online Transactions

Ensuring the security of online transactions is paramount for any e-commerce website. Customers trust your platform with their sensitive information, such as credit card details and personal data. In this section, we will explore essential security measures to protect online transactions in your PHP-based e-commerce application.

1. HTTPS Encryption

Implementing HTTPS (Hypertext Transfer Protocol Secure) is the first and foremost step in securing online transactions. It encrypts the data transmitted between the user's browser and your web server, preventing eavesdropping and data tampering during transmission.

To enable HTTPS, obtain an SSL/TLS certificate from a trusted Certificate Authority (CA) and configure your web server (e.g., Apache or Nginx) to use it. Additionally, set up a secure socket layer for your PHP application.

2. PCI DSS Compliance

If your e-commerce website handles credit card information, you must comply with the Payment Card Industry Data Security Standard (PCI DSS). This standard ensures that cardholder data is stored and transmitted securely.

PCI DSS compliance involves secure data storage, network protection, vulnerability management, access control, and regular security assessments. Use payment gateways that are PCI DSS compliant to offload some of the compliance responsibilities.

3. Payment Gateway Integration

Integrate with reputable and secure payment gateways, such as PayPal, Stripe, or Authorize.Net. These gateways handle payment processing and ensure the security of sensitive payment data. Using a well-established payment gateway can reduce the burden of security compliance on your side.

4. Tokenization

Tokenization is a technique used to replace sensitive data (e.g., credit card numbers) with non-sensitive tokens. When a customer makes a payment, the actual data is securely stored by the payment gateway, and your system only handles tokens. This reduces the risk associated with storing sensitive information.

```
// Example of tokenization

$token = generatePaymentToken($creditCardNumber);
```

5. Two-Factor Authentication (2FA)

Implement Two-Factor Authentication for user accounts, especially during the checkout process. This adds an extra layer of security by requiring users to provide a second form of verification, such as a one-time code sent to their mobile device, in addition to their password.

6. Regular Security Audits

Conduct regular security audits and vulnerability assessments to identify and address potential security weaknesses. Employ security professionals or use automated tools to perform these assessments.

7. Secure Coding Practices

Train your development team to follow secure coding practices. Avoid common vulnerabilities such as SQL injection, cross-site scripting (XSS), and cross-site request forgery (CSRF). Utilize PHP security libraries and frameworks to help prevent these vulnerabilities.

8. Data Encryption

Encrypt sensitive data at rest, such as customer records and order details, in your database. Use strong encryption algorithms and protect encryption keys.

```
// Example of data encryption

$encryptedData = encrypt($sensitiveData, $encryptionKey);
```

9. User Data Protection

Respect user privacy and protect their personal data. Ensure that you have a clear privacy policy and comply with data protection regulations, such as the General Data Protection Regulation (GDPR).

10. Regular Updates

Keep your PHP framework, libraries, and third-party plugins up to date. Developers frequently release security patches, and staying current reduces the risk of known vulnerabilities being exploited.

11. Incident Response Plan

Prepare an incident response plan that outlines how to handle security breaches and data breaches. Swift and effective responses can mitigate the impact of security incidents.

12. Security Training

Educate your employees about security awareness. Phishing attacks and social engineering attempts are common ways that attackers gain access to systems.

Securing online transactions is an ongoing process that requires continuous vigilance and adaptation to emerging threats. By implementing these security measures, you can build trust with your customers and protect their sensitive data, ultimately fostering a secure and successful e-commerce platform.

Section 14.5: Analyzing and Optimizing E-commerce Performance

Performance optimization is crucial for e-commerce websites. Slow loading times and unresponsive pages can lead to a poor user experience and loss of potential customers. In this section, we will explore strategies for analyzing and optimizing the performance of your PHP-based e-commerce platform.

1. Performance Metrics

Before optimizing your e-commerce website, it's essential to establish baseline performance metrics. Use tools like Google PageSpeed Insights, GTmetrix, or New Relic to measure your website's load times, page size, and other performance indicators. Identify areas that need improvement.

2. Caching

Implement caching mechanisms to reduce server load and improve response times. PHP frameworks like Symfony and Laravel offer built-in caching features. Utilize caching for frequently accessed pages, database queries, and assets like images and stylesheets.

```
// Example of caching in Laravel

Cache::remember('products', $minutes, function () {

return Product::all();

});
```

3. Content Delivery Network (CDN)

Use a Content Delivery Network to distribute your website's assets, such as images and scripts, across multiple servers worldwide. CDNs reduce latency by serving content from the server closest to the user's location, improving page load times.

4. Lazy Loading

Implement lazy loading for images and other non-essential content. Lazy loading loads resources only when they come into the user's viewport, reducing initial page load times.

```
<!—Example of lazy loading for images—>

<img data-src="image.jpg" class="lazyload" alt="Product Image">
```

5. Database Optimization

Optimize your database queries to improve performance. Use indexing, query optimization, and caching of frequently accessed database results. Consider denormalizing data for read-heavy operations.

```
—Example of indexing

CREATE INDEX idx_product_name ON products (name);
```

6. Minification and Compression

Minify CSS, JavaScript, and HTML files to reduce their file sizes. Enable server-side compression (gzip or Brotli) to further decrease the size of transferred data, leading to faster page loading.

7. Mobile Optimization

Ensure that your e-commerce website is mobile-friendly. Responsive design and mobile optimization improve the user experience for customers browsing and shopping on smartphones and tablets.

8. Load Testing

Conduct load testing to evaluate how your website performs under heavy traffic conditions. Tools like Apache JMeter and Loader.io can simulate high user loads and help identify bottlenecks.

9. Code Profiling

Use code profiling tools to identify performance bottlenecks within your PHP application. Profilers provide insights into which parts of your code consume the most resources and require optimization.

10. Content Optimization

Optimize product images and descriptions for faster loading. Use appropriate image formats (e.g., WebP), compress images, and provide concise, high-quality content.

```
<!—Example of using the WebP image format—>

<picture>

<source srcset="image.webp" type="image/webp">

<img src="image.jpg" alt="Product Image">

</picture>
```

11. Content Preloading

Preload critical resources like CSS, JavaScript, and fonts to improve perceived page speed. This ensures that essential assets are fetched early, even before they are explicitly requested.

```
<!—Example of content preloading—>

<link rel="preload" href="styles.css" as="style">
```

```
<script src="script.js" defer></script>
```

12. Monitoring and Alerts

Implement monitoring solutions to detect performance issues in real-time. Set up alerts to notify your team when anomalies occur, allowing for immediate intervention.

13. Continuous Optimization

Performance optimization is an ongoing process. Regularly analyze your website's performance metrics, monitor user behavior, and adapt your optimization strategies to evolving user demands and technology trends.

By implementing these performance optimization techniques, you can ensure that your e-commerce platform delivers a fast and responsive shopping experience, ultimately leading to increased customer satisfaction and higher conversion rates.

Chapter 15: PHP 7 and Big Data

In this chapter, we'll explore the intersection of PHP 7 and big data. Big data refers to large and complex datasets that traditional data processing applications struggle to handle. PHP, primarily known for web development, can also play a role in processing and analyzing big data when used in conjunction with the right tools and technologies.

Section 15.1: Introduction to Big Data Concepts

What Is Big Data?

Big data refers to datasets that are too large, diverse, or complex for traditional data processing tools and methods to manage efficiently. These datasets can include structured, semi-structured, or unstructured data from various sources such as social media, sensors, logs, and more. The key characteristics of big data are often summarized using the "3Vs" model:

1. **Volume**: Big data involves a massive amount of data. This can range from gigabytes to petabytes or even exabytes of information.
2. **Velocity**: Data in the big data world is generated rapidly and continuously. It often requires real-time or near-real-time processing.
3. **Variety**: Big data comes in various formats, including structured data (e.g., databases), semi-structured data (e.g., JSON, XML), and unstructured data (e.g., text, images, videos).

Challenges of Big Data

Processing big data presents several challenges, including:

- **Storage**: Storing massive amounts of data efficiently and cost-effectively.

- **Processing**: Analyzing and extracting valuable insights from data in a timely manner.

- **Distribution**: Handling distributed data sources and processing across multiple servers or clusters.
- **Complexity**: Dealing with the variety of data formats and sources.
- **Privacy and Security**: Ensuring the privacy and security of sensitive data.
- **Scalability**: Scaling infrastructure and applications to handle growing data volumes.

Big Data Technologies

To address these challenges, various big data technologies and frameworks have emerged. Some popular ones include:

- **Hadoop**: An open-source framework for distributed storage and processing of large datasets.
- **Apache Spark**: A fast, in-memory data processing engine suitable for big data analytics.
- **NoSQL Databases**: Databases like MongoDB, Cassandra, and Couchbase designed for handling unstructured and semi-structured data.
- **Data Warehouses**: Systems like Amazon Redshift and Google BigQuery optimized for analytical queries on large datasets.
- **Machine Learning**: Big data often intersects with machine learning, allowing businesses to derive predictive insights.

PHP's Role in Big Data

While PHP is not typically the first choice for big data processing due to its interpreted nature and performance limitations compared to languages like Python or Java, it can still play a role in the big data ecosystem. PHP can be used for tasks such as data ingestion, web-based data reporting, and integration with big data pipelines. Additionally, PHP frameworks and libraries can be leveraged to build web-based dashboards and interfaces for big data applications.

In the following sections, we will explore how PHP can be integrated with big data technologies and used effectively in scenarios where it complements the overall data processing workflow.

Section 15.2: PHP in Data Analysis and Processing

PHP, primarily recognized for web development, may not be the first choice for heavy data analysis and processing tasks, especially when dealing with big data. However, there are scenarios where PHP can be employed effectively for data-related tasks, provided it is used in conjunction with appropriate tools and libraries. In this section, we'll explore some ways PHP can be used in data analysis and processing.

PHP for Data Ingestion

One of PHP's strengths is its ability to interact with various data sources and formats. When dealing with big data, it's common to have data coming from diverse sources, such as databases, APIs, log files, and more. PHP's versatility makes it suitable for building data ingestion scripts that fetch, transform, and load data into a central data store or processing pipeline.

For example, you can create PHP scripts that use libraries like Guzzle or cURL to fetch data from web APIs and store it in a database or a distributed storage system. PHP can also parse and process log files generated by applications or servers, extracting valuable information for further analysis.

PHP for Data Transformation

Data transformation is a crucial step in the data processing pipeline. PHP's support for string manipulation, regular expressions, and array handling makes it handy for cleaning, formatting, and transforming data into a usable state.

You can write PHP scripts to perform operations like data cleansing, data enrichment, and data aggregation. These scripts can be integrated into data workflows to ensure that the incoming data is prepared for analysis or storage.

```
// Example: Data cleansing in PHP

$dirtyData = "10,000"; // Data with commas

$cleanData = str_replace(",", "", $dirtyData); // Remove commas

echo $cleanData; // Output: 10000
```

PHP for Reporting and Visualization

PHP can be used to build web-based reporting and visualization tools that allow users to interact with and explore data. Libraries like Chart.js or D3.js can be integrated with PHP to create dynamic and interactive charts and graphs based on the analyzed data.

Web-based dashboards can also be developed using PHP frameworks like Laravel or Symfony. These dashboards can provide real-time insights into data, making it easier for decision-makers to monitor key metrics and trends.

```
// Example: Using Chart.js with PHP data

<?php

$data = [10, 25, 15, 30, 20];

?>

<canvas id="myChart"></canvas>

<script>

var ctx = document.getElementById('myChart').getContext('2d');

var myChart = new Chart(ctx, {

type: 'bar',

data: {

labels: ['Label 1', 'Label 2', 'Label 3', 'Label 4', 'Label 5'],

datasets: [{

label: 'Data',

data: <?php echo json_encode($data); ?>,

backgroundColor: 'rgba(75, 192, 192, 0.2)',

borderColor: 'rgba(75, 192, 192, 1)',

borderWidth: 1

}]

},
```

```
options: {
scales: {
y: {
beginAtZero: true
}
}
}
});
</script>
```

PHP in ETL (Extract, Transform, Load) Workflows

ETL processes are fundamental in data warehousing and data integration. PHP can play a role in ETL workflows, especially when data extraction and transformation involve web-based data sources. PHP scripts can extract data from web APIs, transform it as needed, and load it into data warehouses or databases for further analysis.

In ETL scenarios, PHP can serve as the "Extract" and "Transform" components, working in tandem with other tools or languages for the "Load" phase. Integrating PHP with ETL tools like Apache Nifi or Talend can help streamline data pipelines.

Conclusion

While PHP may not be the primary choice for data analysis and processing, it can be a valuable addition to your data toolkit, especially when handling data ingestion, transformation, reporting, and integration with web-based data sources. When combined with appropriate libraries and tools, PHP can contribute to effective data workflows in the context of big data.

Section 15.3: Integrating PHP with Big Data Technologies

In the era of big data, handling massive volumes of data efficiently is crucial for businesses and organizations. PHP, with its roots in web development, may not be the first choice for big data processing. However, it can still play a role in big data ecosystems when integrated with appropriate technologies and tools. In this section, we'll explore how PHP can be integrated with big data technologies for various data processing tasks.

Apache Hadoop and PHP

Apache Hadoop is a popular framework for distributed storage and processing of large datasets. While Hadoop itself is written in Java, you can interact with Hadoop's HDFS (Hadoop Distributed File System) and submit MapReduce jobs from PHP using libraries or wrappers like PHP-Hadoop.

PHP-Hadoop provides PHP bindings for Hadoop, enabling you to interact with HDFS, submit MapReduce jobs, and access Hadoop's ecosystem from your PHP applications. This integration allows you to leverage Hadoop's scalability and distributed computing capabilities for big data processing.

Apache Spark and PHP

Apache Spark is another powerful framework for big data processing, offering in-memory data processing and support for various data sources. While Spark is primarily associated with Scala and Python, you can use Spark's REST API to submit jobs and access Spark's capabilities from PHP.

Using the Spark REST API, you can create PHP applications that interact with Spark clusters, submit Spark jobs, and retrieve results. This integration enables you to harness the speed and efficiency of Spark for data processing tasks, even from within your PHP-based applications.

PHP and Apache Kafka

Apache Kafka is a distributed streaming platform that is commonly used for real-time data processing and event streaming. PHP can interact with Kafka using libraries like PHP-Rdkafka. With PHP-Rdkafka, you can produce and consume messages from Kafka topics directly from your PHP applications.

This integration is valuable when dealing with real-time data streams or event-driven architectures. PHP can act as a consumer or producer, allowing you to build real-time data processing pipelines or connect PHP applications to Kafka-based data streams.

PHP and Apache Flink

Apache Flink is a stream processing framework designed for big data analytics and real-time processing. While Flink primarily supports Java and Scala, you can use PHP-Flink, a PHP client for Apache Flink, to interact with Flink clusters and submit Flink jobs from PHP.

With PHP-Flink, you can build PHP applications that utilize Flink's stream processing capabilities. This integration is beneficial for scenarios where real-time data analytics or complex event processing is required within PHP applications.

Conclusion

While PHP is not the go-to language for big data processing, it can be integrated effectively with various big data technologies and frameworks. Whether you need to work with Hadoop, Spark, Kafka, or Flink, PHP's flexibility allows you to connect to these systems, enabling your PHP applications to participate in big data workflows and data processing tasks. Integrating PHP with big data technologies can be particularly valuable when your organization relies on PHP for web development and also requires big data processing capabilities.

Section 15.4: Real-time Data Processing with PHP

Real-time data processing is essential in today's fast-paced world, where businesses need to make quick decisions based on incoming data. PHP, traditionally used for web development, can also play a role in real-time data processing when integrated with appropriate tools and technologies. In this section, we'll explore how PHP can be utilized for real-time data processing tasks.

PHP and WebSocket

WebSocket is a communication protocol that enables real-time, bidirectional data exchange between a client and a server. PHP can be used to create WebSocket servers, allowing you to build applications that provide real-time updates to clients. Libraries like Ratchet make it easier to implement WebSocket servers in PHP.

You can use PHP-based WebSocket servers for applications like real-time chat, online gaming, live notifications, or any scenario where low-latency data transmission is crucial. These servers can communicate with clients over WebSocket connections and push data updates in real-time.

```
// Example of a simple WebSocket server in PHP using Ratchet

use Ratchet\Server\IoServer;

use Ratchet\Http\HttpServer;

use Ratchet\WebSocket\WsServer;

use Your\WebSocket\Chat;

require 'vendor/autoload.php';

$server = IoServer::factory(

new HttpServer(

new WsServer(

new Chat()

)

),

8080

);

$server->run();
```

PHP and Apache Kafka

Apache Kafka, as mentioned earlier, is a distributed streaming platform often used for real-time data processing. PHP can interact with Kafka to both produce and consume real-time data streams. By integrating PHP with Kafka, you can create applications that react to incoming data in real-time, making it suitable for scenarios like monitoring, analytics, and event-driven architectures.

```
// Example of producing messages to a Kafka topic using PHP-Rdkafka

$conf = new RdKafka\Conf();

$conf->set('metadata.broker.list', 'localhost:9092');

$producer = new RdKafka\Producer($conf);

$producer->addBrokers('localhost:9092');

$topic = $producer->newTopic('test-topic');

$topic->produce(RD_KAFKA_PARTITION_UA, 0, 'Hello, Kafka!');
```

PHP and Redis Pub/Sub

Redis, a popular in-memory data store, provides a publish/subscribe (Pub/Sub) feature that allows for real-time data distribution. PHP can utilize Redis Pub/Sub to implement real-time messaging and broadcasting systems. Applications can publish messages to channels, and subscribers receive updates in real-time.

```
// Example of publishing a message to a Redis channel using Predis

$redis = new Predis\Client();

$message = json_encode(['event' => 'new_message', 'data' => 'Hello, World!']);

$channel = 'chat';

$redis->publish($channel, $message);
```

PHP and Server-Sent Events (SSE)

Server-Sent Events (SSE) is a simple and efficient technology for real-time data streaming from the server to the client over a single HTTP connection. PHP can generate SSE streams to deliver real-time updates to web clients. SSE is suitable for applications like live dashboards, stock market tickers, or news feeds.

```
// Example of an SSE server in PHP

header('Content-Type: text/event-stream');

header('Cache-Control: no-cache');

while (true) {

$data = ['message' => 'New event data', 'timestamp' => time()];

echo "data: " . json_encode($data) . "\n\n";

flush();

sleep(1); // Adjust the interval as needed

}
```

Conclusion

PHP, with its ability to handle HTTP requests and its support for various communication protocols and data stores, can be integrated effectively into real-time data processing scenarios. Whether you need to implement WebSocket servers, consume data from Kafka, use Redis Pub/Sub, or deliver real-time updates with SSE, PHP can be a valuable tool for building responsive, real-time applications that meet the demands of modern users and businesses. Integrating real-time data processing capabilities into your PHP applications can enhance user experiences, provide timely information, and support data-driven decision-making processes.

Section 15.5: Case Studies in Big Data and PHP Integration

In this section, we'll explore real-world case studies that demonstrate the integration of PHP with big data technologies. These examples showcase how PHP can be used effectively in various industries and scenarios where processing and analyzing large volumes of data are essential.

Case Study 1: E-commerce Recommendation Engine

Industry: E-commerce

Challenge: A large online retailer wanted to improve its product recommendation system to enhance the shopping experience for customers. They needed a solution that could analyze the browsing and purchasing behavior of millions of users in real-time to provide personalized product recommendations.

Solution: PHP was used in combination with big data technologies like Apache Hadoop and Apache Spark. Data collected from user interactions on the website, including clicks, searches, and purchases, was processed and analyzed in real-time. PHP scripts were responsible for handling user requests and displaying recommended products.

```
// Sample PHP code for fetching personalized recommendations

$user = getCurrentUser(); // Get the current user

$recommendedProducts = getRecommendationsForUser($user);
```

Outcome: The integration of PHP with big data allowed the retailer to provide personalized recommendations to users, resulting in increased sales and improved customer satisfaction.

Case Study 2: Healthcare Data Analytics

Industry: Healthcare

Challenge: A healthcare provider needed to analyze and process large volumes of patient data, including electronic health records (EHRs) and medical images, to identify trends, improve patient care, and enhance clinical decision-making.

Solution: PHP was used to develop a web-based application that allowed healthcare professionals to access and analyze patient data securely. Big data technologies like Apache Hadoop and Apache Flink were employed to handle the processing of large datasets. PHP served as the front-end interface, enabling users to interact with and visualize the results of data analysis.

```
// Sample PHP code for querying patient data and displaying analytics

$patient = getPatientInfo($patientId); // Retrieve patient information

$medicalHistory = getMedicalHistory($patientId); // Retrieve medical history

$analysisResults = performDataAnalysis($medicalHistory);
```

Outcome: The integration of PHP and big data technologies enabled healthcare providers to make data-driven decisions, improve patient outcomes, and enhance the quality of care.

Case Study 3: Financial Fraud Detection

Industry: Finance

Challenge: A financial institution needed to detect fraudulent transactions in real-time to prevent financial losses and maintain the trust of its customers. Analyzing vast amounts of transaction data quickly and accurately was critical.

Solution: PHP, combined with big data technologies such as Apache Kafka and Apache Flink, was employed to create a real-time fraud detection system. PHP scripts processed incoming transaction data, and big data platforms handled the analysis of transaction patterns and anomalies.

// Sample PHP code for real-time transaction processing and fraud detection

$transaction = getIncomingTransaction(); *// Receive incoming transaction data*

$isFraudulent = detectFraud($transaction); *// Perform fraud detection*

Outcome: The integration of PHP with big data technologies allowed the financial institution to detect and prevent fraudulent transactions in real-time, safeguarding its financial assets and reputation.

Conclusion

These case studies illustrate the versatility and effectiveness of integrating PHP with big data technologies across different industries. PHP serves as a powerful front-end tool for interacting with users and presenting data, while big data platforms handle the processing and analysis of large datasets. This integration empowers organizations to make data-driven decisions, enhance customer experiences, and achieve their business objectives in an era where big data plays a crucial role in decision-making and innovation.

Chapter 16: PHP 7 for Enterprise Applications

Section 16.1: Designing Enterprise-level Applications

In this section, we will explore the intricacies of designing enterprise-level applications using PHP 7. Enterprises often require robust, scalable, and secure software solutions to meet their complex needs. PHP, with its flexibility and powerful features, can be a valuable tool in building such applications.

Understanding Enterprise Application Requirements

Enterprise applications typically have specific requirements that set them apart from smaller projects. These requirements may include high scalability, reliability, security, and integration with various systems. Before embarking on an enterprise project, it's crucial to thoroughly understand the client's needs and expectations.

Design Principles for Enterprise Applications

1. **Modularization**: Enterprise applications are complex and often comprise multiple modules or components. PHP's support for object-oriented programming and modularization techniques can help in building a structured and maintainable codebase.
2. **Scalability**: Enterprises may experience rapid growth, and their applications must be able to handle increased loads. PHP allows for horizontal scaling, where additional servers can be added to distribute the load effectively.
3. **Security**: Security is paramount in enterprise applications.

Utilize PHP's security features, such as input validation, secure coding practices, and encryption, to safeguard sensitive data and prevent vulnerabilities.

4. **Database Optimization**: Enterprise applications typically interact with large databases. Efficiently design database schemas, use caching mechanisms, and optimize queries to ensure smooth database operations.
5. **Error Handling and Logging**: Implement robust error handling and logging mechanisms to identify and address issues promptly. PHP provides various tools and libraries for effective error management.

PHP Frameworks for Enterprise Development

Several PHP frameworks are well-suited for enterprise-level development. Frameworks like Laravel, Symfony, and Zend Framework provide essential features and components to streamline the development process. They offer built-in support for modularization, security, and scalability.

Integrating with Enterprise Systems

Enterprise applications often need to integrate with existing systems, such as ERP (Enterprise Resource Planning), CRM (Customer Relationship Management), or legacy software. PHP can facilitate integration through APIs, web services, and middleware solutions.

Case Studies: Large-scale PHP Applications

To illustrate the concepts discussed in this section, we will explore real-world case studies of large-scale PHP applications used by prominent enterprises. These case studies will provide insights into how PHP can be effectively utilized to meet the demands of enterprise-level software solutions.

In conclusion, designing enterprise-level applications with PHP 7 requires a deep understanding of the specific requirements, adherence to best practices, and the use of appropriate frameworks and tools. The subsequent sections of this chapter will delve into further details and practical examples to help you master the art of enterprise application development with PHP.

Section 16.2: Scalability and High Availability

Scalability and high availability are two critical aspects of designing enterprise-level applications. Scalability ensures that your application can handle increasing loads and growing user bases, while high availability guarantees that your application remains accessible even in the face of failures. In this section, we'll explore these concepts and how PHP can be used to achieve them.

Scalability

1. **Horizontal vs. Vertical Scaling**: PHP applications can be scaled both horizontally and vertically. Horizontal scaling involves adding more servers to distribute the load, while vertical scaling means upgrading a single server's resources. Depending on your application's needs, you can choose the appropriate scaling strategy.
2. **Load Balancing**: Load balancing is a common technique for achieving scalability. By distributing incoming requests across multiple servers, you can ensure that no single server becomes a bottleneck. PHP can be used in conjunction with load balancers like NGINX or HAProxy to achieve this.
3. **Caching**: Implementing caching mechanisms is crucial for improving scalability. PHP offers various caching

solutions, such as opcode caching (e.g., APCu), object caching (e.g., Memcached, Redis), and full-page caching. These mechanisms can significantly reduce the load on your servers.

4. **Asynchronous Processing**: For tasks that can be offloaded from the main application flow, consider implementing asynchronous processing. PHP can work with message queues like RabbitMQ or Apache Kafka to process background tasks efficiently.

High Availability

1. **Redundancy**: High availability is achieved through redundancy. Have redundant servers, databases, and network connections to eliminate single points of failure. PHP applications can be deployed across multiple servers for redundancy.
2. **Failover Mechanisms**: Implement failover mechanisms that automatically switch to backup systems in case of failures. Load balancers can play a crucial role in directing traffic to healthy servers. PHP applications should be designed to handle failovers gracefully.
3. **Database Replication**: Use database replication techniques like master-slave replication or multi-master setups to ensure database availability. PHP applications can be configured to switch between database servers in case of failures.

PHP and Cloud Services

Cloud platforms like AWS, Google Cloud, and Azure offer tools and services for achieving scalability and high availability. PHP applications can be deployed on these platforms, taking advantage of auto-scaling, load balancers, and managed database services.

Monitoring and Alerts

Monitoring your application's performance and health is essential. Use monitoring tools to collect metrics and set up alerts for critical thresholds. PHP applications can log important events and metrics for analysis.

Case Studies

To illustrate the concepts of scalability and high availability, we'll look at case studies of large-scale PHP applications that have successfully implemented these strategies. These real-world examples will provide insights into how PHP can be used effectively in enterprise environments.

In summary, scalability and high availability are crucial considerations when designing enterprise-level PHP applications. Whether you choose to scale horizontally or vertically, implement caching mechanisms, or leverage cloud services, PHP offers the flexibility and tools needed to build robust and highly available systems.

Section 16.3: Security Considerations for Enterprise Systems

Security is of paramount importance when designing enterprise-level applications. These systems often deal with sensitive data, large user bases, and potential threats from both external and internal sources. In this section, we'll explore the security considerations that PHP developers should keep in mind when building enterprise applications.

Data Encryption and Protection

1. **Data Encryption**: Use encryption techniques like HTTPS (SSL/TLS) to secure data transmission between clients and servers. Additionally, encrypt sensitive data stored in databases to protect it from unauthorized access.
2. **Authentication and Authorization**: Implement strong authentication mechanisms, such as multi-factor authentication (MFA), to verify users' identities. Define strict access controls and authorization policies to ensure that users only have access to the data and functionality they need.

Vulnerability Management

1. **Regular Audits and Scans**: Perform security audits and vulnerability scans regularly to identify and address potential weaknesses in your application's code and infrastructure. Tools like OWASP ZAP and Nessus can help in this regard.
2. **Patch Management**: Keep all software components, including the PHP runtime, web server, and database, up to date with the latest security patches. Vulnerabilities in these components can be exploited by attackers.

Security Best Practices

1. **Secure Coding Standards**: Follow secure coding standards and practices to prevent common vulnerabilities such as SQL injection, cross-site scripting (XSS), and cross-site request forgery (CSRF). Tools like PHP CodeSniffer with security rulesets can assist in enforcing coding standards.

2. **Input Validation**: Sanitize and validate user input to prevent malicious data from entering your application. PHP provides functions like filter_var and mysqli_real_escape_string for input validation and SQL injection prevention.

Logging and Monitoring

1. **Security Logging**: Implement comprehensive logging of security-relevant events, including failed login attempts, access to sensitive data, and potential security breaches. Monitoring tools can help detect anomalies and trigger alerts.

Disaster Recovery and Incident Response

1. **Backup and Recovery**: Regularly back up your application's data and configurations. Create disaster recovery plans to ensure minimal downtime in the event of a breach or system failure.
2. **Incident Response Plan**: Develop an incident response plan that outlines the steps to be taken in case of a security incident. This plan should include communication procedures and actions to contain and mitigate the incident.

Employee Training and Awareness

1. **Security Training**: Train your development and operations teams in security best practices. Awareness among employees is crucial to prevent accidental security breaches.

Compliance and Regulations

1. **Compliance**: Ensure that your application complies with industry-specific regulations and standards, such as GDPR, HIPAA, or PCI DSS, if applicable. These regulations may have specific requirements for data protection and security.

Case Studies

To illustrate these security considerations, we'll examine case studies of PHP-based enterprise applications that have successfully implemented robust security measures. These examples will demonstrate how PHP can be used securely in large-scale and high-risk environments.

In summary, security is a fundamental aspect of designing and maintaining enterprise-level PHP applications. By following best practices, staying informed about emerging threats, and regularly assessing and improving security measures, you can build and operate secure systems that protect sensitive data and maintain the trust of your users and stakeholders.

Section 16.4: Integrating with Enterprise Databases

Enterprise-level PHP applications often rely on robust database systems to manage and store large volumes of data efficiently. In this section, we'll explore the key considerations and best practices for integrating PHP applications with enterprise databases.

Choosing the Right Database System

Selecting an appropriate database system is crucial for the success of your enterprise application. Consider the following factors when making your choice:

1. **Scalability**: Ensure that the chosen database can scale horizontally and vertically to accommodate growing data volumes and user loads.
2. **Data Consistency**: Maintain data consistency and integrity by selecting a database that supports transactions and adheres to the ACID (Atomicity, Consistency, Isolation, Durability) properties.
3. **Performance**: Evaluate the database's performance capabilities, including query optimization, indexing, and caching mechanisms.
4. **High Availability**: Implement database clustering and replication to ensure high availability and fault tolerance.
5. **Security**: Choose a database system that provides robust security features, including authentication, authorization, and encryption.

Database Connection and ORM

When working with enterprise databases in PHP, consider the following best practices:

1. **Connection Pooling**: Use connection pooling to efficiently manage database connections and reduce overhead, especially in high-traffic environments.
2. **Object-Relational Mapping (ORM)**: Consider using an ORM library like Doctrine or Eloquent to abstract database interactions and simplify complex queries.
3. **Database Abstraction Layers**: Implement a database

abstraction layer to make your code more portable across different database systems.

SQL Query Optimization

Efficient database queries are critical for maintaining application performance. Follow these optimization guidelines:

1. **Indexing**: Properly index database tables to speed up query execution. Analyze query execution plans to identify areas for improvement.
2. **Caching**: Implement query caching to reduce the load on the database server and improve response times.

Data Migration and Versioning

As your enterprise application evolves, you may need to perform data migrations and versioning:

1. **Migration Tools**: Use migration tools like Phinx or Laravel's built-in migration system to manage database schema changes over time.
2. **Version Control**: Keep database schema changes under version control to track and document modifications.

Backup and Recovery

Develop a robust backup and recovery strategy to safeguard your enterprise database:

1. **Regular Backups**: Schedule regular database backups and store them securely offsite.
2. **Point-in-Time Recovery**: Implement point-in-time recovery to restore the database to a specific state in case of

data corruption or errors.

Monitoring and Performance Tuning

Continuous monitoring and performance tuning are essential for maintaining a healthy database system:

1. **Monitoring Tools**: Use database monitoring tools to track performance metrics, detect anomalies, and receive alerts.
2. **Query Optimization**: Regularly review and optimize database queries for improved performance.
3. **Resource Scaling**: Scale database resources, such as CPU and memory, based on demand to ensure optimal performance.

Security

Security remains a top priority when working with enterprise databases:

1. **Access Control**: Implement fine-grained access control by defining user roles and permissions in the database.
2. **Data Encryption**: Encrypt sensitive data at rest and in transit to protect it from unauthorized access.

Case Studies

To illustrate these database integration considerations, we'll explore case studies of enterprise PHP applications that have effectively integrated with enterprise-grade databases. These examples will highlight how proper database management contributes to the success of large-scale applications.

In conclusion, integrating PHP applications with enterprise databases requires careful planning, selection of the right database system, efficient query optimization, and robust security measures. By following these best practices and learning from real-world case studies, you can build and maintain enterprise-grade PHP applications that meet the data management needs of your organization.

Section 16.5: Case Studies: Large-scale PHP Applications

In this section, we will delve into case studies of large-scale PHP applications that have successfully handled significant traffic and complex requirements. These real-world examples will highlight the architecture, technologies, and best practices employed to achieve scalability, high availability, and performance.

1. Facebook

Description: Facebook is one of the largest social media platforms globally, serving billions of users. PHP played a pivotal role in its early development, and while the company has developed its own programming language, Hack, based on PHP, PHP remains a significant part of Facebook's technology stack.

Key Takeaways:

- **HipHop Virtual Machine (HHVM)**: Facebook developed HHVM to improve PHP's performance. HHVM is a just-in-time (JIT) compiler that translates PHP code into machine code, significantly boosting execution speed.

- **Scalability**: Facebook's infrastructure relies on thousands of servers distributed globally to manage user data and interactions. They employ various techniques for load balancing and content delivery to handle the immense user base.

2. Wikipedia

Description: Wikipedia, the world's largest online encyclopedia, relies heavily on PHP for its server-side scripting. It serves millions of users daily and hosts an extensive database of articles.

Key Takeaways:

- **MediaWiki**: Wikipedia uses MediaWiki, a PHP-based open-source wiki software, which provides the platform for collaborative editing and content management.

- **Caching**: To handle the high volume of requests, Wikipedia employs caching mechanisms extensively. This reduces the load on the database and web servers and improves response times.

3. Slack

Description: Slack is a popular team collaboration platform used by businesses worldwide. PHP is used in various parts of Slack's infrastructure.

Key Takeaways:

- **Leveraging PHP for Microservices**: Slack uses PHP in microservices, enabling developers to build and deploy independently scalable components.

- **Real-time Messaging**: Slack relies on WebSockets for real-time messaging, and PHP is used for building and managing WebSocket servers.

4. Etsy

Description: Etsy is an e-commerce platform specializing in handmade and vintage items. PHP powers many parts of Etsy's website and backend systems.

Key Takeaways:

- **Horizontal Scaling**: Etsy uses PHP alongside other technologies to handle traffic spikes during peak shopping seasons. Their infrastructure can dynamically scale based on demand.
- **Data Sharding**: Etsy employs data sharding techniques to distribute database load effectively and enhance database performance.

5. Badoo

Description: Badoo is a dating-focused social network with over 400 million registered users. PHP has been a core part of their technology stack since its inception.

Key Takeaways:

- **Custom PHP Framework**: Badoo developed its own PHP framework, LVOOP (Large Volume Object-Oriented PHP), to cater to the specific requirements of their platform.
- **Big Data Processing**: Badoo uses PHP for processing and analyzing large volumes of user data to provide recommendations and improve user experiences.

6. Magento

Description: Magento is a popular e-commerce platform, and PHP is at the heart of its development. It caters to businesses of all sizes, and many online stores use Magento.

Key Takeaways:

- **Modularity**: Magento's architecture is highly modular, allowing businesses to customize their online stores. PHP is used for developing custom extensions and themes.
- **Elasticsearch Integration**: Many Magento installations integrate Elasticsearch, a search and analytics engine, to enhance product search capabilities.

These case studies illustrate the versatility and scalability of PHP in building and maintaining large-scale applications. PHP's adaptability, combined with the right architectural decisions and technologies, can lead to the successful development and operation of complex, high-traffic platforms.

Chapter 17: PHP 7 and Machine Learning

Section 17.1: Fundamentals of Machine Learning

Machine Learning (ML) is a field of artificial intelligence that focuses on the development of algorithms and models that allow computer systems to learn and make predictions or decisions without being explicitly programmed. It has gained immense popularity and practical applications across various domains, including healthcare, finance, marketing, and more. In this section, we will explore the fundamentals of machine learning and its relevance to PHP 7.

What is Machine Learning?

Machine Learning is a subset of artificial intelligence (AI) that enables computers to learn from data and improve their performance on specific tasks over time. The core idea is to develop algorithms that can identify patterns, make predictions, or perform tasks based on input data without being explicitly programmed for each task.

Key Concepts in Machine Learning

1. Data

Data is the foundation of machine learning. It can come in various forms, including text, numbers, images, and more. Machine learning models use data to learn patterns and make predictions.

2. Features

Features are specific attributes or characteristics extracted from the data that are relevant to the problem at hand. Feature selection and engineering are crucial in preparing data for machine learning.

3. Labels

In supervised learning, data is labeled with the correct output or target variable. The model learns from labeled data to make predictions on new, unlabeled data.

4. Algorithms

Machine learning algorithms are the mathematical and computational techniques used to train models. Popular algorithms include linear regression, decision trees, neural networks, and more.

5. Training

Training is the process of feeding the algorithm with labeled data and adjusting its internal parameters to minimize prediction errors. It involves optimization techniques like gradient descent.

6. Testing and Evaluation

After training, models are tested on new, unseen data to evaluate their performance. Metrics like accuracy, precision, recall, and F1-score are used to assess model quality.

7. Model Deployment

Once a model performs well in testing, it can be deployed in real-world applications to make predictions or automate tasks.

Machine Learning Libraries in PHP

While Python is a dominant language for machine learning, PHP also offers libraries and tools for ML tasks. Some notable PHP ML libraries and tools include:

- **PHP-ML**: A machine learning library for PHP that provides various algorithms for classification, regression, clustering, and more.
- **Tenserflow PHP**: A PHP extension that allows interaction with Google's TensorFlow framework, enabling deep learning capabilities.
- **H2O.ai**: An open-source machine learning platform with a PHP client that provides advanced ML algorithms and autoML.
- **Mahout PHP**: A PHP extension for Apache Mahout, which offers scalable machine learning algorithms for big data processing.

Use Cases of Machine Learning in PHP

Machine learning can be applied to various PHP-based applications and scenarios, such as:

- **Recommendation Systems**: Implementing recommendation engines for e-commerce or content platforms to enhance user experiences.

- **Natural Language Processing (NLP)**: Analyzing and processing text data for sentiment analysis, chatbots, or language translation.

- **Predictive Analytics**: Building predictive models for forecasting, fraud detection, or customer churn prediction.

- **Image Recognition**: Developing image classification or object detection models for applications like image tagging or security.

Machine learning in PHP opens up opportunities to create intelligent and data-driven applications. As we delve deeper into this chapter, we will explore how to integrate machine learning into PHP projects and leverage the power of predictive modeling and data analysis.

Section 17.2: Integrating Machine Learning Libraries with PHP

Integrating machine learning libraries with PHP allows developers to harness the power of pre-built algorithms and tools for various tasks without having to implement everything from scratch. In this section, we will explore how to integrate machine learning libraries into PHP projects, enabling us to leverage the capabilities of these libraries for tasks like data processing, model training, and predictions.

PHP-ML: A Machine Learning Library for PHP

One of the most popular machine learning libraries for PHP is PHP-ML. It provides a wide range of machine learning algorithms, making it suitable for tasks such as classification, regression, clustering, dimensionality reduction, and more. Here are the key steps to get started with PHP-ML:

1. **Installation**: You can install PHP-ML using Composer, the PHP package manager. Simply run the following command in your project directory:

```
composer require php-ai/php-ml
```

1. **Data Preparation**: Prepare your data by collecting and cleaning it. Data should be in a format suitable for machine learning, with features and labels if it's a supervised task.
2. **Selecting and Training a Model**: Choose an appropriate machine learning algorithm for your task. PHP-ML provides various algorithms like Decision Trees, Support Vector Machines, Naive Bayes, and more. Train your model using the training data.
3. **Testing and Evaluation**: After training, test your model's performance on a separate set of data to evaluate its accuracy and effectiveness. PHP-ML offers tools to calculate metrics like accuracy, precision, recall, and F1-score.
4. **Prediction**: Once your model is trained and evaluated, you can use it to make predictions on new, unseen data. This is often the primary goal of machine learning.

TensorFlow PHP: Interacting with TensorFlow

If you're interested in deep learning and neural networks, TensorFlow is a popular framework developed by Google. You can use TensorFlow with PHP using the TensorFlow PHP extension. Here's how you can get started:

1. **Install TensorFlow**: First, you need to install TensorFlow on your server or local environment. Follow the official installation instructions for your platform.
2. **Install TensorFlow PHP Extension**: You can use the tensorflow/tensorflow Composer package to interact with TensorFlow in PHP. Install it with:

```
composer require tensorflow/tensorflow
```

1. **Use TensorFlow in PHP**: With TensorFlow and the PHP extension installed, you can use PHP to build, train, and deploy deep learning models. This is particularly useful for tasks like image recognition, natural language processing, and more.

H2O.ai: Open Source Machine Learning Platform

H2O.ai is an open-source machine learning platform with an easy-to-use interface and a powerful API. While it is not native to PHP, you can use PHP's HTTP capabilities to interact with H2O.ai's REST API. This allows you to access advanced machine learning algorithms and autoML capabilities for tasks like classification, regression, and anomaly detection.

Leveraging Machine Learning in PHP Projects

Integrating machine learning libraries with PHP opens up a world of possibilities for your projects. You can enhance your web applications with intelligent features, automate decision-making processes, and gain valuable insights from data.

Here are some practical applications of machine learning in PHP projects:

- **E-commerce Recommendations**: Implement product recommendations based on user behavior and preferences.
- **Customer Support Chatbots**: Create chatbots that can understand and respond to user inquiries intelligently.
- **Predictive Analytics**: Build predictive models to forecast demand, sales, or customer churn.
- **Image Recognition**: Develop applications that can recognize and classify images uploaded by users.
- **Text Analysis**: Perform sentiment analysis, topic modeling, or text summarization for content-rich platforms.

As you explore machine learning in PHP, keep in mind that the choice of library and algorithm depends on your specific use case and project requirements. Experimentation and iterative development are key to harnessing the full potential of machine learning in your PHP applications.

Section 17.3: Building Predictive Models

with PHP

Building predictive models with PHP is a powerful way to make data-driven decisions and automate processes. In this section, we'll explore the process of creating predictive models using machine learning techniques in PHP. Whether you want to predict customer behavior, forecast sales, or make recommendations, predictive models can be valuable assets.

Data Preparation

The first step in building predictive models is data preparation. You need clean and well-structured data to train and test your models effectively. Data preparation typically includes tasks like:

- Data Cleaning: Removing or filling missing values, handling outliers, and addressing data quality issues.

- Feature Engineering: Creating relevant features from the existing data that can improve model performance.

- Data Splitting: Dividing your dataset into training and testing sets to evaluate model accuracy.

Choosing a Machine Learning Algorithm

Selecting an appropriate machine learning algorithm depends on your problem. Common algorithms for predictive modeling include:

- Linear Regression: Used for predicting numerical values (regression problems).

- Logistic Regression: Suitable for binary classification problems.

• Decision Trees: Good for both classification and regression tasks.

• Random Forests: An ensemble method that combines multiple decision trees for better performance.

• Support Vector Machines (SVM): Effective for classification tasks, especially when dealing with complex decision boundaries.

• Neural Networks: Deep learning models that excel in tasks like image recognition and natural language processing.

Model Training and Evaluation

Once you've chosen an algorithm, you need to train and evaluate your model. Here's a general outline of the process:

1. **Training**: Use the training dataset to train your model. The model learns patterns and relationships within the data.
2. **Validation**: Assess the model's performance on a validation dataset that it hasn't seen during training. Adjust hyperparameters if needed.
3. **Testing**: Finally, evaluate the model's performance on a separate testing dataset to estimate its real-world performance.

PHP Libraries for Predictive Modeling

There are several PHP libraries that you can use for building predictive models:

1. PHP-ML

PHP-ML[1] is a versatile machine learning library for PHP that provides implementations of various algorithms. Here's a basic example of how to train a linear regression model using PHP-ML:

```
use Phpml\Regression\LeastSquares;

// Sample data

$samples = [[1], [2], [3], [4]];

$targets = [2, 4, 6, 8];

// Create and train the model

$regression = new LeastSquares();

$regression->train($samples, $targets);

// Predict a value

$prediction = $regression->predict([5]);

echo "Prediction: $prediction";
```

2. PHP-ML Integration with Databases

PHP-ML can be used in conjunction with database libraries like PDO to build models based on data stored in databases. You can retrieve data from a database, preprocess it, and train your model as shown in the example above.

1. https://php-ml.org/

3. Integration with Data Visualization

Visualization libraries like PHPlot[2] can help you visualize the results of your predictive models. You can create charts and graphs to gain insights into your data and model performance.

Real-World Applications

Predictive modeling has a wide range of real-world applications. Here are a few examples:

- **Predictive Analytics in E-commerce**: Predict customer preferences and recommend products.
- **Financial Forecasting**: Forecast stock prices, currency exchange rates, or credit risk.
- **Healthcare Predictions**: Predict patient outcomes, disease progression, or hospital resource utilization.
- **Demand Forecasting**: Predict demand for products to optimize supply chain management.
- **Energy Consumption Forecasting**: Forecast energy consumption for efficient resource allocation.

Remember that building predictive models often involves an iterative process of refining the model, selecting the right features, and fine-tuning hyperparameters. Additionally, data privacy and ethical considerations should be taken into account when working with sensitive data for predictive modeling.

Section 17.4: PHP in Data Mining and

2. http://www.phplot.com/

Analysis

Data mining and analysis play a crucial role in extracting valuable insights from large datasets. PHP can be a useful tool for data mining and analysis tasks, especially when combined with appropriate libraries and tools. In this section, we'll explore how PHP can be employed for data mining, data manipulation, and analysis.

Data Mining Techniques

Data mining involves the discovery of patterns, trends, and useful information from vast datasets. PHP can be used in conjunction with libraries like phpMyAdmin[3] and phpMiner for various data mining tasks, such as:

1. **Association Rule Mining**: Discovering relationships between different data items in a database, often used in market basket analysis.
2. **Clustering**: Grouping similar data points together, allowing for better understanding of data structure and segmentation.
3. **Classification**: Building models to categorize data into predefined classes or labels, making predictions based on historical data.
4. **Time Series Analysis**: Analyzing and forecasting time-dependent data, which is common in finance, economics, and weather forecasting.

Data Manipulation with PHP

PHP provides a wide range of functions and libraries to manipulate and preprocess data efficiently. Whether you are working with CSV

3. https://www.phpmyadmin.net/

files, databases, or web scraping, PHP can help. Here's an example of reading and processing data from a CSV file:

```
// Read data from a CSV file

$csvFile = 'data.csv';

$csvData = array_map('str_getcsv', file($csvFile));

// Extract the headers

$headers = array_shift($csvData);

// Process and analyze the data

foreach ($csvData as $row) {

// Perform data analysis or manipulation here

// Example: Calculate the average of a specific column

$average = array_sum($row) / count($row);

echo "Average: $average\n";

}
```

Libraries and Tools

PHP can be integrated with various libraries and tools to enhance data mining and analysis capabilities:

- **PHPExcel**: A library for working with Excel files, useful for data import/export.
- **phpMyAdmin**: A popular tool for managing MySQL databases, which includes data analysis features.

- **R and PHP Integration**: You can integrate R, a powerful statistical computing language, with PHP using packages like rPHP.

Visualizing Data

Data visualization is an essential aspect of data analysis. While PHP itself is not primarily designed for creating complex data visualizations, you can utilize JavaScript libraries like D3.js[4] or Chart.js[5] for interactive charts and graphs in web applications.

Real-World Applications

Data mining and analysis with PHP find applications in various domains:

- **Business Analytics**: Analyzing sales data, customer behavior, and market trends to make informed business decisions.

- **Social Media Analysis**: Extracting insights from social media posts and user interactions.

- **Healthcare**: Analyzing patient records and medical data for disease prediction and treatment recommendations.

- **E-commerce**: Recommender systems to suggest products to customers based on their browsing and purchase history.

- **Finance**: Analyzing financial data for risk assessment, fraud detection, and investment strategies.

---

4. https://d3js.org/

5. https://www.chartjs.org/

In conclusion, PHP, when combined with the right tools and libraries, can be a versatile choice for data mining and analysis tasks. It allows you to process and manipulate data efficiently, extract valuable insights, and drive data-driven decision-making in various domains.

Section 17.5: Real-world Applications of Machine Learning in PHP

Machine learning (ML) is a transformative field that has found applications across various industries. In this section, we will explore real-world applications of machine learning using PHP as a programming language. These applications demonstrate the versatility and power of PHP when integrated with ML libraries and tools.

Fraud Detection in Banking

One of the critical applications of machine learning in the banking sector is fraud detection. PHP can be used in combination with ML libraries such as scikit-learn[6] or TensorFlow[7] to build models that detect fraudulent transactions. ML algorithms can analyze transaction data, identify unusual patterns, and raise alerts for potential fraud. PHP-based web applications can then interact with these models to provide real-time fraud detection for users.

```
// Example using scikit-learn in Python for fraud detection

# Import libraries

import pandas as pd
```

6. https://scikit-learn.org/

7. https://www.tensorflow.org/

```
from sklearn.model_selection import train_test_split

from sklearn.ensemble import RandomForestClassifier

from sklearn.metrics import accuracy_score

# Load and preprocess data

data = pd.read_csv('transaction_data.csv')

X = data.drop(columns=['fraud'])

y = data['fraud']

# Split data into training and testing sets

X_train, X_test, y_train, y_test = train_test_split(X, y, test_size=0.2, random_state=42)

# Build a Random Forest classifier

model = RandomForestClassifier(n_estimators=100, random_state=42)

model.fit(X_train, y_train)

# Predict on test data

y_pred = model.predict(X_test)

# Evaluate the model

accuracy = accuracy_score(y_test, y_pred)

print(f'Accuracy: {accuracy}')
```

Recommendation Systems for E-commerce

E-commerce platforms often employ recommendation systems to enhance user experience and boost sales. PHP-based applications can integrate with recommendation models to provide personalized product suggestions. Machine learning algorithms analyze user behavior, purchase history, and product interactions to generate tailored recommendations.

```
// PHP code to fetch personalized product recommendations

$userID = $_SESSION['user_id'];

// Query the ML recommendation model to get product suggestions for the user

$suggestedProducts = getRecommendationsFromMLModel($userID);

// Display the recommended products on the website

foreach ($suggestedProducts as $product) {

echo "Recommended: {$product['name']} - {$product['price']} USD<br>";

}
```

Healthcare Diagnosis and Prediction

Machine learning plays a crucial role in healthcare for disease diagnosis and prediction. PHP-based healthcare systems can integrate ML models that analyze patient data, medical records, and test results to assist healthcare professionals in making accurate diagnoses and predicting disease outcomes.

```
// PHP code to integrate a disease prediction model
```

```
$patientData = fetchPatientData($_POST['patient_id']);

$prediction = predictDiseaseOutcome($patientData);

// Display the prediction to the healthcare professional

echo "Predicted Disease Outcome: $prediction";
```

Natural Language Processing in Content Analysis

Natural Language Processing (NLP) is a subfield of machine learning that deals with text and language. PHP-based content management systems can utilize NLP models to analyze and categorize textual content. This can be applied in sentiment analysis, content tagging, and automated content recommendations.

```
// PHP code to perform sentiment analysis on user-generated content

$userReview = $_POST['user_review'];

$sentiment = performSentimentAnalysis($userReview);

if ($sentiment === 'positive') {

echo "Thank you for your positive review!";

} elseif ($sentiment === 'negative') {

echo "We're sorry to hear about your experience. Please contact our support team.";

} else {

echo "Your review has been received.";

}
```

Customer Support Chatbots

Customer support chatbots powered by machine learning can efficiently handle customer inquiries and provide instant responses. PHP-based chatbots can integrate with ML models to understand and respond to customer queries effectively, improving user satisfaction.

```
// PHP code for a customer support chatbot

$userQuery = $_POST['user_query'];

// Use ML model to determine the intent and generate a response

$intent = determineUserIntent($userQuery);

$response = generateChatbotResponse($intent);

// Display the chatbot's response to the user

echo "Chatbot: $response";
```

These real-world applications highlight how PHP, when combined with machine learning, can be used to solve complex problems and enhance various aspects of business and technology. As machine learning continues to advance, its integration with PHP offers exciting opportunities for innovation and automation in diverse industries.

Chapter 18: Best Practices in PHP 7 Development

In this chapter, we will explore best practices in PHP 7 development. Following coding standards and adopting best practices can make your PHP code more maintainable, efficient, and secure. Whether you are working on a small project or a large-scale application, these practices will help you write high-quality PHP code.

Section 18.1: Code Organization and Structure

Organizing your PHP code is essential for maintaining a clean and structured codebase. Proper code organization makes it easier for you and your team to understand, modify, and extend your PHP applications. Here are some best practices for code organization and structure:

1. Directory Structure:

- **Separation of Concerns:** Divide your code into separate directories based on their functions. Common directories include "controllers," "models," "views," and "libraries."

- **PSR-4 Autoloading:** Follow the PSR-4 autoloading standard to autoload your classes efficiently. This standard maps namespaces to directory structures, making it easy to locate and include classes.

- **Configuration Files:** Store configuration settings in dedicated files. Avoid hardcoding configuration values directly into your code.

- **Assets:** Keep assets such as JavaScript, CSS, and images in separate directories and serve them statically for better performance.

2. Namespace and Class Organization:

- **Namespacing:** Use namespaces to prevent naming conflicts and improve code readability. Follow a consistent naming convention for namespaces.

- **Single Responsibility Principle (SRP):** Ensure that each class has a single responsibility. This promotes code reusability and maintainability.

- **PSR-1 and PSR-2:** Follow the PSR-1 and PSR-2 coding standards for class naming, file organization, and coding style.

3. Code Comments and Documentation:

- **DocBlocks:** Use PHPDoc comments to document your code. Describe class methods, properties, and parameters. Tools like phpDocumentor[8] can generate documentation from DocBlocks.

- **Inline Comments:** Add inline comments to clarify complex logic or non-obvious code sections. Explain the "why" behind the code, not just the "how."

- **Keep Comments Updated:** Maintain and update comments when you make code changes. Outdated comments can mislead developers.

8. https://www.phpdoc.org/

4. Separation of Logic:

- **MVC Architecture:** Follow the Model-View-Controller (MVC) architecture to separate application logic, presentation, and data. This improves code maintainability and allows for easier collaboration among developers.

- **Avoid Mixing HTML and PHP:** Minimize the mixing of PHP code and HTML. Use template engines or view files to separate presentation from PHP logic.

5. Dependency Management:

- **Composer:** Use Composer[9] for dependency management. It simplifies the installation and management of external libraries and packages.

- **Version Control:** Use a version control system like Git to track changes in your codebase and collaborate with others.

6. Error Handling:

- **Error Reporting:** Set appropriate error reporting levels in your development environment to catch and address issues early.

- **Custom Error Handling:** Implement custom error handlers to gracefully handle errors and exceptions, providing meaningful error messages to users and developers.

9. https://getcomposer.org/

By adhering to these code organization and structure best practices, you can create PHP applications that are easier to maintain, collaborate on, and extend. Well-organized code is the foundation for writing reliable and scalable PHP applications.

Section 18.2: Advanced Coding Standards and Practices

In this section, we'll delve deeper into advanced coding standards and practices in PHP 7 development. Following these practices will not only improve the quality of your code but also make it more maintainable, efficient, and secure.

1. PSR-12: Extended Coding Style Guide

While PSR-2 provides a basic coding style guide, PSR-12 extends it to cover more aspects of coding standards. It addresses issues like brace placement, switch statements, and use statements. Adhering to PSR-12 ensures a consistent and easily readable code style.

2. Type Hinting and Return Types

PHP 7 introduced return type declarations and type hinting. Use these features to specify the expected data types for function arguments and return values. This enhances code clarity and helps catch type-related errors early.

```
// Type hinting for function arguments

function calculateTotal(float $price, int $quantity): float {

return $price * $quantity;

}
```

```
// Return type declaration
function getUserData(int $userId): ?array {
// ...
}
```

3. Code Refactoring

Regularly review and refactor your code to eliminate redundancy, improve efficiency, and enhance readability. Tools like PHP_CodeSniffer and PHPStan[10] can help identify areas that need improvement.

4. Design Patterns

Familiarize yourself with common design patterns like Singleton, Factory, Observer, and Dependency Injection. These patterns provide proven solutions to recurring design problems and improve code organization.

5. SOLID Principles

The SOLID principles (Single Responsibility, Open/Closed, Liskov Substitution, Interface Segregation, Dependency Inversion) offer guidelines for writing maintainable and extensible code. Apply these principles to create more modular and flexible PHP applications.

10. https://phpstan.org/

6. Testing and Test-Driven Development (TDD)

Adopt Test-Driven Development (TDD) practices to write tests before implementing code. Use PHPUnit or other testing frameworks to automate unit and integration tests. TDD ensures that your code meets requirements and helps identify issues early in development.

7. Code Reviews

Regular code reviews with peers or team members can catch issues that might be missed during development. Code reviews promote knowledge sharing and maintain code quality.

8. Dependency Injection

Implement Dependency Injection to decouple components and make your code more testable. Avoid tightly coupling classes, as it makes code maintenance and testing challenging.

```
class OrderProcessor {
private $mailer;
public function __construct(Mailer $mailer) {
$this->mailer = $mailer;
}
// ...
}
```

9. Version Control Best Practices

Follow version control best practices like creating meaningful commit messages, branching strategies, and documenting changes. Use Git workflows like Gitflow or GitHub Flow to collaborate efficiently.

10. Code Reviews and Continuous Integration

Integrate code reviews into your development process and set up continuous integration (CI) pipelines. CI tools like Jenkins, Travis CI, or GitHub Actions automate testing, code quality checks, and deployments.

11. Documentation

Maintain comprehensive documentation for your code, including API documentation, user guides, and README files. Tools like phpDocumentor[11] can generate documentation from inline comments.

By embracing these advanced coding standards and practices, you can elevate your PHP 7 development skills and contribute to the creation of robust and maintainable applications. Well-structured, efficient, and well-documented code is crucial for the long-term success of any PHP project.

---

11. https://www.phpdoc.org/

Section 18.3: Code Refactoring and Maintenance

Code refactoring and maintenance are essential aspects of PHP 7 development that contribute to code quality, readability, and long-term sustainability. In this section, we will explore strategies and best practices for effective code refactoring and maintenance.

1. Why Code Refactoring?

Code refactoring is the process of restructuring existing code without altering its external behavior. It serves several purposes:

- **Enhancing Code Quality**: Refactoring improves code readability, maintainability, and overall quality.
- **Bug Fixing**: Refactoring can help identify and fix bugs or issues in the code.
- **Performance Optimization**: It can lead to performance improvements by eliminating bottlenecks and inefficiencies.
- **Maintainability**: Well-refactored code is easier to maintain and extend.

2. Code Smells

Code smells are signs that indicate the need for refactoring. Common code smells include:

- **Duplicated Code**: Repeated sections of code should be extracted into functions or methods.

- **Long Methods/Functions**: Large methods or functions should be divided into smaller, more focused ones.
- **Large Classes**: Classes with too many responsibilities should be split or refactored into smaller classes.
- **Deep Nesting**: Excessive levels of nesting in conditionals or loops should be reduced for clarity.
- **Comments**: Overly commented code may indicate the need for more self-explanatory code.

3. Refactoring Techniques

Here are some commonly used refactoring techniques:

- **Extract Method/Function**: Break down large methods/functions into smaller ones that perform specific tasks.

```
// Before refactoring

function calculateTotal($price, $quantity) {

$subtotal = $price * $quantity;

$tax = $subtotal * 0.10;

return $subtotal + $tax;

}

// After refactoring
```

```
function calculateSubtotal($price, $quantity) {

return $price * $quantity;

}

function calculateTax($subtotal) {

return $subtotal * 0.10;

}

function calculateTotal($price, $quantity) {

$subtotal = calculateSubtotal($price, $quantity);

$tax = calculateTax($subtotal);

return $subtotal + $tax;

}
```

- **Replace Conditional with Polymorphism**: Instead of complex conditional statements, use polymorphism to handle different cases.

- **Rename Variables and Functions**: Choose descriptive names for variables and functions to improve code readability.

- **Remove Dead Code**: Eliminate unused or redundant code to reduce clutter and confusion.

- **Code Duplication**: Identify duplicated code and encapsulate it in functions, methods, or classes.

4. Version Control and Git

Utilize version control systems like Git to track changes, collaborate with others, and easily revert to previous code versions if needed. Create meaningful commit messages and follow branching strategies.

5. Testing and Continuous Integration

Maintain a suite of unit tests and integration tests to ensure that code changes do not introduce new bugs. Set up continuous integration (CI) pipelines to automate testing and code quality checks.

6. Documentation

Keep documentation up to date. Documenting code changes, API endpoints, and usage instructions helps developers understand and use the code effectively.

7. Regular Code Reviews

Perform regular code reviews with team members to identify issues, provide feedback, and ensure code quality and consistency.

Effective code refactoring and maintenance practices are crucial for keeping your PHP 7 projects healthy and sustainable over time. Regularly reviewing and improving your codebase leads to more maintainable, efficient, and bug-free applications.

Section 18.4: Documentation and Readability

Documentation and code readability are essential aspects of PHP 7 development that contribute to code maintainability and collaboration. In this section, we will explore strategies for effective documentation and improving code readability.

1. Code Comments

Comments are an integral part of documentation, helping developers understand the code's purpose and functionality. Here are some best practices for using code comments:

- **Function and Method Comments**: Include comments at the beginning of functions and methods to describe their purpose, input parameters, and return values.

```
/**

* Calculates the total price.

*

* @param float $price The price of the item.

* @param int $quantity The quantity of items.

* @return float The total price.

*/

function calculateTotal($price, $quantity) {

// Calculate the total price.
```

```
$subtotal = $price * $quantity;

$tax = $subtotal * 0.10;

return $subtotal + $tax;

}
```

• **Class Comments**: Provide an overview of classes, explaining their role and usage.

```
/**

* Represents a product in the e-commerce system.

*/

class Product {

// Class implementation.

}
```

• **Inline Comments**: Use inline comments sparingly and only when necessary to clarify complex logic or non-obvious behavior.

```
// Check if the user is logged in.

if ($loggedIn) {

// Perform some action for authenticated users.

}
```

2. Inline Documentation

PHPDoc is a popular format for inline documentation. It allows you to generate documentation from your codebase using tools like PHPDocumentor. Here's an example:

```
/**

* Represents a product in the e-commerce system.

*

* @property int $id The unique identifier.

* @property string $name The product name.

* @property float $price The product price.

*/

class Product {

// Class implementation.

}
```

3. Self-Explanatory Code

Write code that is self-explanatory and follows best practices for readability:

- Use meaningful variable and function names.
- Follow consistent coding conventions and indentation.
- Avoid excessive nesting and complex logic.

4. External Documentation

Apart from in-code documentation, consider creating external documentation using tools like Sphinx or Markdown files. This documentation can include project overviews, installation guides, and usage instructions.

5. README Files

Include a well-structured README file in your project repository. A good README should provide an introduction, installation instructions, usage examples, and any other relevant information.

6. Versioning Documentation

Ensure that documentation is versioned alongside your code. When making significant changes to the codebase, update the documentation to reflect those changes.

7. Collaboration Tools

Use collaboration tools like Git and platforms like GitHub or GitLab to manage documentation updates collaboratively. Encourage team members to contribute to documentation improvements.

8. Continuous Integration for Documentation

Automate documentation generation and checks as part of your continuous integration (CI) pipeline. Ensure that documentation remains accurate and up to date with code changes.

By focusing on code comments, inline documentation, self-explanatory code, and external documentation, you can significantly improve the readability and maintainability of your PHP 7 projects. Effective documentation practices make it easier for developers to understand, use, and contribute to your codebase.

Section 18.5: Community and Continuing Education

In the dynamic world of PHP 7 development, community involvement and continuous learning are key to staying up-to-date with the latest trends, best practices, and advancements in the field. This section explores the importance of being an active part of the PHP community and emphasizes the significance of ongoing education.

1. Engage in PHP Communities

Participating in PHP communities, online forums, and discussion groups can be immensely beneficial. Communities like the PHP FIG (Framework Interoperability Group), Stack Overflow, and PHP-related subreddits provide platforms for developers to seek help, share knowledge, and collaborate on projects. Engaging with these communities can help you:

- Solve coding challenges and troubleshoot issues.
- Learn from experienced developers and gain insights into best practices.
- Contribute to open-source projects and enhance your portfolio.
- Stay informed about the latest PHP updates and trends.

2. Attend PHP Conferences and Meetups

PHP conferences and local meetups offer opportunities to connect with fellow developers, industry experts, and thought leaders. These events feature informative talks, workshops, and networking sessions that can enrich your knowledge and broaden your professional network. Some popular PHP conferences include PHP[tek], PHP UK, and SunshinePHP.

3. Continuous Learning

The field of web development, including PHP, evolves rapidly. To stay competitive, it's crucial to invest in continuous learning. Here are some ways to do that:

- Online Courses: Enroll in online courses and tutorials offered by platforms like Udemy, Coursera, and edX. These courses cover a wide range of PHP topics, from beginner to advanced.

- Books: Invest in PHP books authored by experts in the field. Reading books dedicated to PHP or web development can deepen your understanding.

- Coding Challenges: Solve coding challenges on platforms like LeetCode and HackerRank to sharpen your problem-solving skills and keep your coding skills sharp.

- Experiment and Build: Create personal projects or contribute to open-source projects to apply your knowledge and gain practical experience.

- Explore New Technologies: PHP is often used in conjunction with other technologies. Explore related technologies such as JavaScript frameworks, databases, and cloud platforms.

4. Version Updates

Stay informed about PHP version updates and migration guides. As PHP evolves, new features and improvements are introduced, and older versions become deprecated. Keeping your projects up-to-date ensures security, performance, and compatibility.

5. Security Awareness

Security is paramount in web development. Stay updated on PHP security best practices and vulnerabilities. Joining mailing lists or forums dedicated to PHP security can help you stay vigilant and protect your applications from threats.

6. Mentorship and Collaboration

Consider seeking mentorship or becoming a mentor yourself. Collaborating with more experienced developers or guiding newcomers can be mutually beneficial and accelerate your learning.

7. Contribute to the PHP Ecosystem

Contributing to the PHP ecosystem by developing extensions, libraries, or tools not only benefits the community but also enhances your expertise and reputation. Engage in open-source projects and consider contributing to PHP itself on platforms like GitHub.

By actively participating in the PHP community, pursuing continuous education, and staying updated on PHP developments, you can ensure your PHP 7 development skills remain relevant and continue to evolve with the industry. The PHP community is known for its camaraderie and willingness to share knowledge, making it an excellent environment for both novice and experienced developers to thrive.

Chapter 19: PHP 7 and the Future of Web Development

Section 19.1: Current Trends in Web Development

Web development is an ever-evolving field, and staying abreast of current trends is vital for PHP developers looking to remain competitive. In this section, we'll explore some of the latest trends shaping the world of web development as of the knowledge cutoff date in January 2022.

1. Responsive Web Design

Responsive web design remains a cornerstone of modern web development. With an increasing number of users accessing websites on various devices, ensuring that your web applications are responsive and adaptable to different screen sizes is imperative. CSS frameworks like Bootstrap and Flexbox have played a significant role in simplifying responsive design.

2. Progressive Web Apps (PWAs)

PWAs continue to gain traction. These web applications offer a native app-like experience in the browser. They load quickly, work offline, and can be installed on a user's device, blurring the lines between web and mobile app development. PHP developers can leverage frameworks like Symfony and Laravel to build PWAs.

3. Single Page Applications (SPAs)

SPAs, powered by JavaScript frameworks like React, Vue.js, and Angular, have become increasingly popular. They provide a seamless user experience by loading content dynamically, reducing page refreshes, and offering a more app-like feel. PHP can be used as a backend for SPAs to handle data processing and API interactions.

4. Serverless Computing

Serverless architecture, offered by cloud providers like AWS Lambda and Azure Functions, simplifies server management. PHP developers can leverage serverless platforms to run code in response to events without the need to manage servers. This approach can be cost-effective and scalable for certain applications.

5. API-First Development

API-first development involves designing the application's API before building the frontend or backend. This approach facilitates efficient collaboration among frontend and backend developers and allows for the development of multiple client applications (web, mobile, IoT) that consume the same API. PHP frameworks like Lumen and Slim are well-suited for building APIs.

6. Jamstack Architecture

Jamstack (JavaScript, APIs, and Markup) has gained popularity due to its focus on decoupling the frontend from the backend. PHP can be used to build APIs that serve content to Jamstack-based websites, combining the flexibility of PHP with the benefits of static site generators.

7. Containerization and Microservices

Containerization technologies like Docker and orchestration platforms like Kubernetes are revolutionizing how applications are deployed and managed. PHP applications can be containerized and orchestrated, making it easier to scale and manage complex applications.

8. Artificial Intelligence (AI) and Machine Learning (ML)

Integrating AI and ML into web applications is becoming more accessible. PHP developers can utilize libraries and APIs for tasks like natural language processing, image recognition, and recommendation systems. This trend opens up opportunities for creating intelligent and personalized web experiences.

9. Web Assembly (Wasm)

Web Assembly allows running high-performance code written in languages like C, C++, and Rust in web browsers. While PHP is not directly compatible with Wasm, developers can explore new possibilities by integrating it with PHP applications for tasks requiring high computational power.

10. Accessibility and Inclusivity

Web accessibility (a11y) and inclusivity are gaining attention. It's essential for developers to create web applications that are usable by people with disabilities. PHP developers can follow best practices and use accessibility tools to ensure their applications are inclusive.

Staying informed about these trends and incorporating relevant technologies and practices into your PHP development toolkit can help you build modern, competitive, and future-proof web applications. As the web development landscape continues to evolve, PHP remains a versatile and powerful tool for crafting a wide range of digital experiences.

Section 19.2: PHP's Role in the Evolving Web Landscape

As the web development landscape continues to evolve, PHP's role remains significant. While new technologies and languages emerge, PHP maintains its relevance and continues to power a substantial portion of the web. In this section, we'll explore PHP's role in the evolving web landscape, highlighting its strengths and how it fits into modern web development.

PHP's Continued Popularity

PHP has a long history and a massive user base. Many existing websites and applications rely on PHP, making it indispensable. Despite the rise of alternative languages, PHP continues to be a popular choice for web development.

Versatility and Scalability

PHP is versatile and can be used for various types of web projects. Whether you're building a simple blog or a complex e-commerce platform, PHP can handle it. Moreover, PHP scales well, and with the right architecture and optimization techniques, it can power high-traffic websites and applications.

Integration with Modern Technologies

PHP can integrate seamlessly with modern web technologies. It can work alongside JavaScript frameworks like React and Vue.js, allowing developers to build dynamic and interactive user interfaces. PHP's ability to serve as a backend for these frameworks is a testament to its adaptability.

APIs and Microservices

As the trend towards microservices and API-first development grows, PHP is well-suited to play a role in this architecture. PHP can be used to create RESTful APIs or GraphQL endpoints, enabling frontend and mobile applications to communicate with the backend efficiently.

Frameworks and Libraries

PHP has a robust ecosystem of frameworks and libraries that simplify web development. Popular frameworks like Laravel, Symfony, and Yii provide tools and conventions that streamline development and promote best practices.

Serverless PHP

Serverless computing has gained popularity, and PHP is not left behind. Developers can use serverless platforms like AWS Lambda or Azure Functions to execute PHP code in a serverless manner. This approach offers cost-effectiveness and scalability for certain use cases.

Future-Focused PHP Versions

The PHP community actively develops and updates the language. With each new version, PHP introduces performance improvements, security enhancements, and new features. Staying up-to-date with the latest PHP versions ensures that developers can leverage the best PHP has to offer.

PHP in AI and Machine Learning

While PHP is not typically associated with AI and machine learning, it can play a role in integrating AI capabilities into web applications. Developers can use PHP to create APIs that interact with AI services or integrate machine learning libraries into PHP projects.

Community Support

PHP has a strong and active community of developers. Online forums, documentation, and open-source contributions ensure that developers have access to resources and assistance when needed. The community's vitality contributes to PHP's longevity.

In conclusion, PHP continues to thrive and evolve within the ever-changing web development landscape. Its versatility, scalability, and adaptability make it a valuable tool for a wide range of web projects. Whether you're building traditional websites, progressive web apps, or APIs for modern applications, PHP remains a relevant and reliable choice. Embracing PHP's strengths and integrating it with other technologies is key to building successful web applications in the future.

Section 19.3: Future Technologies and PHP

As technology continually advances, it's essential to explore how PHP fits into the landscape of future technologies. PHP, with its long-standing history, strong community, and adaptability, remains relevant as developers look ahead to what the future holds.

Embracing Modern Paradigms

PHP has embraced modern programming paradigms. Object-oriented programming (OOP) is a prime example. While PHP started as a procedural language, it has evolved to support OOP fully. This adaptability allows developers to create well-structured and maintainable codebases, aligning with modern development practices.

Asynchronous and Non-blocking PHP

As web applications become more complex and demand real-time interactions, asynchronous and non-blocking programming models gain importance. While PHP traditionally follows a synchronous model, libraries and extensions like ReactPHP enable asynchronous PHP, making it suitable for building responsive and scalable applications that handle multiple concurrent requests efficiently.

```
// Example using ReactPHP

$loop = React\EventLoop\Factory::create();

$loop->addTimer(2, function () {

echo "Hello, after 2 seconds!\n";
```

```
});
$loop->addTimer(1, function () {
echo "Hello, after 1 second!\n";
});
$loop->run();
```

PHP for Web Assembly (Wasm)

Web Assembly is an emerging technology that allows running code written in multiple languages directly in web browsers at near-native speed. While PHP is traditionally a server-side language, efforts are underway to enable PHP to run within the browser using Web Assembly. This opens up new possibilities for web applications that can offload certain tasks to the client-side, enhancing user experiences.

```
// Future PHP running in the browser (Wasm)
$phpCode = 'echo "Hello, Web Assembly!";';
$wasmInstance = new WebAssembly\Instance(
new WebAssembly\Module(wasm_compile_php($phpCode))
);
$wasmInstance->exports->main();
```

PHP and Web APIs

APIs (Application Programming Interfaces) have become the backbone of modern web applications, enabling communication between various services and platforms. PHP's role in this ecosystem continues to expand, as developers use it to create RESTful APIs, GraphQL endpoints, and other web services. Future PHP versions may include enhancements to make API development even more straightforward.

```
// Creating a simple RESTful API in PHP

$app = new Slim\App();

$app->get('/api/data', function (Request $request, Response $response) {

$data = ['message' => 'Hello, API!'];

return $response->withJson($data);

});

$app->run();
```

PHP and Machine Learning

Machine learning (ML) and artificial intelligence (AI) are driving innovation in various industries. PHP's role in this domain may involve integrating machine learning models and libraries into web applications. PHP developers can leverage pre-trained models for tasks like natural language processing, image recognition, and predictive analytics.

```
// Integrating Python-based ML models with PHP

$pythonScript = 'machine_learning.py';

$command = escapeshellcmd("python $pythonScript");

$output = shell_exec($command);
```

```
echo $output;
```

Preparing for Future PHP Versions

The PHP community actively develops and maintains the language. To stay relevant, it's crucial for developers to keep up with the latest PHP versions and features. Additionally, contributing to PHP's open-source development or participating in community discussions can help shape the language's future.

In conclusion, PHP's adaptability and evolving ecosystem position it well for the future of web development. Embracing modern paradigms, exploring asynchronous programming, leveraging Web Assembly, enhancing web API capabilities, integrating machine learning, and staying involved in the PHP community are essential strategies for PHP developers to prepare for the exciting developments on the horizon.

Section 19.4: PHP and Web Assembly (Wasm)

Web Assembly, often abbreviated as Wasm, is a groundbreaking technology that extends the capabilities of web browsers by enabling the execution of code written in various programming languages at near-native speed. While PHP has traditionally been a server-side scripting language, recent developments aim to bring PHP into the realm of client-side web development using Web Assembly. In this section, we'll explore the intersection of PHP and Web Assembly, discussing its potential and providing insights into its implementation.

Understanding Web Assembly

Web Assembly is a binary instruction format designed to run on web browsers alongside JavaScript. It offers a portable and efficient compilation target for high-level programming languages. Instead of relying solely on JavaScript, which is an interpreted language, Web Assembly allows you to execute code written in languages like C, C++, Rust, and now, potentially, PHP.

Why Use PHP with Web Assembly?

The integration of PHP with Web Assembly holds several advantages:

1. **Performance**: Web Assembly code executes at near-native speed, making it ideal for computationally intensive tasks. By offloading certain operations to Web Assembly, you can significantly improve the performance of web applications.
2. **Client-Side Logic**: PHP traditionally runs on the server, but with Web Assembly, you can execute PHP code on the client-side. This opens up new possibilities for creating interactive web applications with client-side PHP logic.
3. **Cross-Platform Compatibility**: Web Assembly runs on various web browsers, making it a cross-platform solution. Your PHP code can work consistently across different browsers without compatibility issues.

Potential Use Cases

While the integration of PHP with Web Assembly is in its early stages, it holds promise for several use cases:

1. **Client-Side Scripting**: You can use Web Assembly to run PHP code in the browser, enabling dynamic interactions

without the need for frequent server requests. For example, you can perform client-side form validation, generate dynamic charts, or manipulate DOM elements using PHP.

2. **Cross-Platform Desktop Applications**: Web Assembly, combined with tools like Electron, allows you to build cross-platform desktop applications with PHP as the core logic. This approach leverages PHP's familiarity while expanding its reach beyond web development.
3. **Offline Web Applications**: Web Assembly enables the creation of offline web applications that can continue to function even without an internet connection. PHP can power the logic of these applications, making them versatile and responsive.
4. **High-Performance Web Games**: For web-based games and simulations, Web Assembly's performance benefits can be a game-changer. PHP can be used for game logic and server communication while leveraging Web Assembly for rendering and real-time interactions.

Exploring PHP and Web Assembly

To explore PHP and Web Assembly, you'll need to consider PHP compilers or transpilers that can convert PHP code into Web Assembly-compatible code. While this area is still evolving, some experimental projects and tools are emerging within the PHP community.

Here's a simplified example of how Web Assembly can be used with PHP (note that this example is highly simplified for demonstration purposes):

```
// Future PHP running in the browser (Web Assembly)

$phpCode = 'echo "Hello, Web Assembly!";';
```

```
$wasmInstance = new WebAssembly\Instance(

new WebAssembly\Module(wasm_compile_php($phpCode))

);

$wasmInstance->exports->main();
```

In this code snippet, we envision a future scenario where PHP code is compiled to Web Assembly and executed in the browser. While this technology is not yet widely available, it showcases the potential for PHP in client-side web development.

Conclusion

Web Assembly is a transformative technology that brings new possibilities to web development. While PHP's primary domain has been server-side scripting, the integration of PHP with Web Assembly presents exciting opportunities for client-side scripting, cross-platform applications, offline web experiences, and high-performance web games. Developers interested in this intersection should keep an eye on emerging tools and projects that enable PHP to run efficiently in the Web Assembly environment.

Section 19.5: Preparing for Future PHP Versions

As PHP continues to evolve, it's essential for developers to stay up-to-date with the latest changes and prepare for future PHP versions. In this section, we'll discuss strategies for ensuring your PHP codebase remains compatible with upcoming releases and take advantage of new features and improvements.

Staying Informed

To prepare for future PHP versions, it's crucial to stay informed about the PHP development roadmap. The official PHP website and community forums are valuable sources of information. Additionally, following PHP-related blogs, newsletters, and participating in online discussions can help you keep track of upcoming changes.

Keeping Your Codebase Up-to-Date

One of the primary tasks in preparing for future PHP versions is ensuring that your codebase is up-to-date with current PHP best practices. This includes:

1. **Updating Deprecated Features**: PHP often marks certain functions, features, or syntax as deprecated before removing them in future versions. Be proactive in updating your code to use recommended alternatives.
2. **Code Refactoring**: Periodically review your codebase for opportunities to improve efficiency, readability, and adherence to coding standards. Code refactoring can make future updates easier and more efficient.
3. **Dependency Management**: Ensure that third-party libraries, frameworks, and packages used in your project are also up-to-date and compatible with future PHP versions. Consider using dependency management tools like Composer to simplify this process.

PHP Version Compatibility

Maintaining compatibility with multiple PHP versions can be challenging, especially when new PHP releases introduce breaking changes. Here are some strategies to manage compatibility effectively:

1. **Version Checks**: Use conditional checks to determine the PHP version your code is running on. This allows you to implement version-specific solutions or fallbacks when necessary.

```
if (version_compare(PHP_VERSION, '7.4', '>=')) {
// Code for PHP 7.4 and later
} else {
// Code for older PHP versions
}
```

1. **Continuous Integration**: Implement continuous integration (CI) pipelines that test your code against different PHP versions. Services like Travis CI or GitHub Actions can automate this process and notify you of compatibility issues.
2. **Polyfills and Compatibility Libraries**: Consider using polyfills or compatibility libraries that provide modern functionality on older PHP versions. These can help bridge the gap between different PHP releases.

Feature Adoption

Embracing new features and improvements introduced in PHP versions can enhance the functionality, security, and performance of your applications. However, it's essential to adopt new features gradually and test thoroughly to ensure they don't introduce unexpected issues.

Community Engagement

Active participation in the PHP community can provide valuable insights into upcoming changes and best practices. Attend PHP conferences, join relevant forums and mailing lists, and contribute to open-source projects to stay connected and informed.

Conclusion

Preparing for future PHP versions is a proactive approach to ensure the longevity and competitiveness of your PHP-based projects. By staying informed, keeping your codebase up-to-date, managing compatibility, adopting new features thoughtfully, and engaging with the PHP community, you can navigate the evolving PHP landscape effectively and continue to deliver high-quality applications to your users.

Chapter 20: Case Studies and Real-world Applications

In the final chapter of this book, we delve into various case studies and real-world applications of PHP. By exploring both successful and failed PHP projects across different industry sectors, we can gain valuable insights into the practical application of PHP in various scenarios. This chapter provides a glimpse into the diverse range of projects that PHP can be used for, offering lessons, best practices, and inspiration for developers and businesses alike.

Section 20.1: Successful PHP Projects

In this section, we will examine a selection of successful PHP projects that have made a significant impact in their respective domains. These case studies highlight the versatility and capabilities of PHP in delivering solutions across various industries. Let's take a closer look at some notable examples:

1. Facebook

Facebook, one of the world's largest social media platforms, was initially built using PHP. The platform's early codebase was primarily written in PHP, and it played a crucial role in Facebook's rapid growth. Although Facebook has evolved its technology stack over the years, PHP remains a foundational part of its history.

2. WordPress

WordPress is a popular content management system (CMS) that powers millions of websites worldwide. It is built on PHP and MySQL, making it a versatile and customizable platform for bloggers, businesses, and developers. WordPress's success as an open-source project is a testament to PHP's capabilities in web development.

3. Magento

Magento is a leading e-commerce platform used by businesses of all sizes to create online stores. It is built with PHP and provides robust e-commerce features, scalability, and customization options. Magento's success in the e-commerce industry showcases PHP's suitability for building complex and high-performance applications.

4. Slack

Slack, a widely used collaboration platform for teams, relies on PHP for various backend services. PHP plays a significant role in handling real-time messaging, user authentication, and data storage in Slack's architecture. This demonstrates PHP's capabilities in supporting real-time communication and large-scale applications.

5. Wikipedia

Wikipedia, the world's largest online encyclopedia, is powered by MediaWiki, which is written in PHP. PHP's flexibility and ease of use make it an excellent choice for building collaborative platforms like Wikipedia. The platform's success highlights PHP's role in supporting knowledge-sharing initiatives.

6. Laravel

Laravel is a modern PHP framework known for its elegant syntax and developer-friendly features. It has gained popularity in the web development community and has been used in numerous successful projects. Laravel's success showcases PHP's adaptability for building modern web applications.

These case studies demonstrate the diverse applications of PHP across various domains, from social media and e-commerce to collaboration and content management. They also underscore PHP's role in powering some of the most prominent websites and applications on the internet.

In the next sections, we'll explore lessons learned from failed PHP projects, PHP's relevance in different industry sectors, and its potential for startups and small businesses. Through these real-world examples, you'll gain a deeper understanding of PHP's strengths and opportunities for growth in the ever-evolving landscape of web development.

Section 20.2: Lessons from Failed PHP Projects

While PHP has powered numerous successful projects, it's essential to acknowledge that not all PHP endeavors have yielded favorable outcomes. Examining the lessons learned from failed PHP projects can provide valuable insights into avoiding common pitfalls and making informed decisions in your development journey. Here, we explore some key factors contributing to the failure of PHP projects:

1. Poor Project Planning

One of the most common reasons for PHP project failure is inadequate project planning. Rushing into development without a clear roadmap, defined objectives, or a well-structured project plan can lead to scope creep, missed deadlines, and budget overruns. To avoid this, invest time in thorough project planning, requirement analysis, and setting achievable milestones.

// Example: Define project milestones

```
$projectMilestones = [
'Requirements Gathering',
'System Design',
'Development Phase 1',
'Testing and Quality Assurance',
'Development Phase 2',
'User Acceptance Testing',
'Deployment and Maintenance',
];
```

2. Inadequate Testing and Quality Assurance

Neglecting proper testing and quality assurance (QA) processes can lead to project failure. Bugs, security vulnerabilities, and performance issues may go unnoticed, resulting in an unreliable system. Implement comprehensive testing strategies, including unit testing, integration testing, and user acceptance testing, to identify and address issues early in the development lifecycle.

```
// Example: PHPUnit test case
class MyTest extends PHPUnit_Framework_TestCase {
public function testAddition() {
$result = 1 + 1;
$this->assertEquals(2, $result);
}
```

```
}
```

3. Insufficient Security Measures

Security breaches can have devastating consequences for PHP projects. Failing to implement robust security measures, such as input validation, data encryption, and access control, can leave your application vulnerable to attacks. Stay updated on security best practices and regularly audit your code for vulnerabilities.

```
// Example: Input validation for preventing SQL injection

$userInput = $_POST['username'];

$cleanInput = mysqli_real_escape_string($dbConnection, $userInput);

$query = "SELECT * FROM users WHERE username = '$cleanInput'";
```

4. Lack of Scalability Planning

PHP projects can outgrow their initial capacity if not designed with scalability in mind. A failure to anticipate increased traffic and data volume may result in performance bottlenecks and downtime. Incorporate scalability considerations into your architecture, such as load balancing, caching, and database optimization.

```
// Example: Implementing Memcached for caching

$memcached = new Memcached();

$memcached->addServer('localhost', 11211);

$key = 'cached_data_key';

$data = $memcached->get($key);
```

```
if (!$data) {
// Fetch data from the database
$data = fetchDataFromDatabase();
// Store data in cache
$memcached->set($key, $data, 3600); // Cache for 1 hour
}
```

5. Outdated PHP Versions and Dependencies

Using outdated PHP versions and dependencies can lead to compatibility issues and security vulnerabilities. Always keep your PHP environment and libraries up to date to benefit from performance improvements and security patches.

```
// Example: Updating Composer dependencies
composer update
```

6. Ineffective Communication

Poor communication among team members and stakeholders can hinder project progress. Misunderstandings, conflicting priorities, and a lack of transparency can lead to project derailment. Establish clear communication channels, regular status updates, and collaborative tools to foster effective teamwork.

```
// Example: Sending project status updates via email or project management tools
$email = 'team@example.com';
$subject = 'Project Status Update';
```

```
$message = 'Dear Team, Here is the latest project status:';

mail($email, $subject, $message);
```

Learning from these common pitfalls and failures can help you make informed decisions, mitigate risks, and increase the likelihood of success in your PHP projects. By addressing these challenges proactively and adopting best practices, you can navigate the complexities of PHP development more effectively.

Section 20.3: PHP and Web Assembly

Web Assembly (Wasm) is a binary instruction format designed to execute code at near-native speed in web browsers. It enables high-performance, portable, and safe execution of applications on web pages, and PHP developers have started exploring its potential. Here, we'll delve into the relationship between PHP and Web Assembly.

Understanding Web Assembly

Web Assembly is not a replacement for JavaScript but rather a complement to it. It allows developers to write code in languages like C, C++, and Rust and compile it to run in web browsers alongside JavaScript. This opens up new possibilities for web applications, including running complex computational tasks, games, and multimedia applications with near-native performance.

Web Assembly operates within a sandboxed environment, ensuring security and preventing direct access to system resources. It provides a common runtime for different languages, making it easier to integrate code written in multiple languages into a single web application.

PHP and Web Assembly Integration

While PHP is traditionally a server-side scripting language, there are experimental projects and tools that aim to bring PHP to the client-side via Web Assembly. These projects involve compiling PHP code into Web Assembly modules, allowing it to execute directly in the browser.

One of the challenges in PHP-Wasm integration is dealing with PHP's server-side nature and its reliance on server resources like file system access and databases. Client-side PHP, running in a browser, lacks direct access to these resources. However, developers have explored solutions like providing mock server APIs or using technologies like IndexedDB for local storage.

```
// Example: Using IndexedDB for local storage in client-side PHP
if ('indexedDB' in window) {
const dbPromise = indexedDB.open('myDatabase', 1);
dbPromise.onupgradeneeded = function (event) {
const db = event.target.result;
const objectStore = db.createObjectStore('data', { keyPath: 'id' });
objectStore.createIndex('name', 'name', { unique: false });
};
dbPromise.onsuccess = function (event) {
const db = event.target.result;
const transaction = db.transaction('data', 'readwrite');
const objectStore = transaction.objectStore('data');
```

```
// Perform CRUD operations on local data
};
}
```

Use Cases and Limitations

The integration of PHP with Web Assembly opens up interesting use cases, such as creating interactive web applications that leverage PHP's capabilities on the client side. Developers can explore scenarios like real-time data processing, client-side data manipulation, and dynamic web applications.

However, it's important to note that client-side PHP-Wasm is still experimental and not suitable for all PHP applications. The technology is evolving, and developers should be aware of its limitations, including the lack of direct server access and potential performance bottlenecks.

Preparing for the Future

While the adoption of PHP and Web Assembly is in its early stages, it represents an exciting development in web technology. Developers interested in exploring this intersection should monitor emerging tools and libraries, as well as stay informed about the latest advancements in Web Assembly support in web browsers.

As the web development landscape evolves, PHP developers can leverage their existing skills to explore new horizons and contribute to the ever-changing world of web technology.

Section 20.4: PHP for Startups and Small Businesses

PHP has played a significant role in the success of many startups and small businesses. Its versatility, ease of use, and cost-effectiveness have made it an attractive choice for companies looking to establish their online presence, build web applications, and manage their websites. In this section, we will explore why PHP is a valuable tool for startups and small businesses.

Cost-Effective Development

One of the primary reasons PHP is favored by startups and small businesses is its cost-effectiveness. PHP is an open-source scripting language, which means there are no licensing fees associated with its use. This cost advantage allows startups and small businesses to allocate their limited resources to other critical aspects of their operations, such as marketing and growth.

PHP also offers compatibility with various databases, many of which are open source as well. This synergy reduces the overall cost of development and maintenance. Additionally, PHP has a large and active community that provides free resources, libraries, and frameworks, further lowering development costs.

Rapid Development

Startups often operate in fast-paced environments, where the ability to develop and iterate on products quickly is essential. PHP's simple and intuitive syntax, along with its extensive libraries and frameworks, enables rapid development of web applications and websites. This agility allows startups to bring their ideas to market faster and make adjustments based on user feedback and market changes.

```
// Example: Creating a simple PHP web application

<?php

$message = "Hello, World!";

echo $message;

?>
```

Scalability

While startups may begin with limited resources, their goal is often to grow and expand their customer base. PHP offers scalability options that allow businesses to start small and gradually increase their infrastructure as needed. This scalability is achieved through various means, such as load balancing, database optimization, and caching mechanisms.

Access to Skilled Developers

PHP has been around for over two decades, resulting in a large pool of skilled PHP developers. For startups and small businesses, this means access to a talent pool of professionals who can quickly understand their requirements and contribute to their projects. Whether hiring in-house developers or outsourcing development work, finding PHP expertise is relatively straightforward.

Ecosystem of Tools and Services

The PHP ecosystem includes a wide range of tools, services, and platforms that simplify various aspects of web development. Content management systems (CMS) like WordPress, e-commerce solutions like WooCommerce, and cloud hosting providers that support PHP applications make it easier for startups to create and manage their online presence without extensive technical knowledge.

Community Support and Resources

The PHP community is known for its supportiveness and willingness to share knowledge. Startups and small businesses can benefit from online forums, blogs, tutorials, and documentation that help solve common issues and challenges. Additionally, the frequent updates and improvements in PHP and its related technologies ensure that businesses can stay competitive in the evolving digital landscape.

In conclusion, PHP is an excellent choice for startups and small businesses looking to build a robust online presence and develop web applications efficiently. Its cost-effectiveness, rapid development capabilities, scalability, access to skilled developers, and rich ecosystem of tools and resources make it a valuable asset for businesses with limited resources and ambitious growth goals. By leveraging PHP, startups can turn their ideas into successful online ventures.

Section 20.5: The Future of PHP in Web Development

The future of PHP in web development holds exciting possibilities and challenges. PHP has evolved significantly since its inception, and it continues to adapt to the changing landscape of web development. In this section, we'll explore the potential directions PHP may take in the coming years.

PHP 8 and Beyond

As of my last knowledge update in January 2022, PHP 8 was the latest major release, introducing numerous improvements and new features. PHP's core development team has been proactive in enhancing the language's performance, type system, and capabilities. It's likely that PHP will continue to receive updates and refinements, further solidifying its position as a modern scripting language.

PHP's roadmap may include features such as improved JIT (Just-In-Time) compilation, enhanced support for asynchronous programming, and better interoperability with other languages. These additions would make PHP more competitive in handling complex and high-performance applications.

Frameworks and Libraries

PHP's ecosystem of frameworks and libraries is vast and continually evolving. Popular PHP frameworks like Laravel, Symfony, and Yii have been instrumental in streamlining web application development. Expect these frameworks to remain active, incorporating new features and best practices as the web development landscape evolves.

Moreover, the PHP community frequently releases new packages and libraries to address specific needs. These community-driven efforts contribute to PHP's versatility and adaptability.

Web Assembly (Wasm)

Web Assembly is an emerging technology that allows running code written in languages other than JavaScript in web browsers. While PHP primarily executes server-side, the ability to compile PHP to Web Assembly could open new possibilities for client-side web development. This would enable developers to share code between the server and client seamlessly.

PHP and Microservices

Microservices architecture is gaining prominence due to its flexibility and scalability benefits. PHP can be a viable choice for building microservices, especially when combined with lightweight frameworks and containerization technologies like Docker. PHP's ability to handle HTTP requests efficiently makes it well-suited for microservices that serve specific functions within a larger application.

PHP and Serverless Computing

Serverless computing abstracts infrastructure management, allowing developers to focus solely on writing code. PHP's stateless nature aligns with the serverless paradigm, making it a candidate for serverless applications. The PHP community may explore how to optimize PHP for serverless platforms like AWS Lambda and Azure Functions.

Sustainability and Security

With the growing emphasis on sustainability and security in web development, PHP will likely continue to improve in these areas. Sustainability includes optimizing resource usage, reducing energy consumption, and minimizing environmental impact. Security enhancements may involve stricter default security settings and tools for vulnerability detection.

Education and Adoption

PHP's popularity among beginners may result in more educational resources, courses, and tutorials for aspiring developers. As PHP remains accessible and approachable, it will continue to serve as a gateway for newcomers to the world of web development.

In conclusion, PHP's future in web development is bright and dynamic. The language will continue to evolve, adapting to emerging technologies and trends while remaining accessible to developers of all levels. PHP's strong community, extensive ecosystem, and historical significance ensure that it will play a vital role in shaping the future of web development for years to come. Developers and businesses alike should keep a close eye on PHP's evolution and leverage its capabilities to create innovative web solutions.

www.ingramcontent.com/pod-product-compliance
Lightning Source LLC
LaVergne TN
LVHW090303210926
848480LV00001B/109

* 9 7 9 8 2 2 4 1 2 5 5 8 6 *